Perspectives in Reading No. 14

PARENTS AND READING

Compiled and Edited by

Carl B. Smith

Indiana University

Prepared by the Joint Committee on Parents and Reading
sponsored by the
International Reading Association and the
National Conference of Parents and Teachers

ira

INTERNATIONAL READING ASSOCIATION

Newark, Delaware 19711

INTERNATIONAL READING ASSOCIATION

OFFICERS
1971-1972

Copyright 1971 by the
International Reading Association, Inc.
Library of Congress Catalog Card Number 74-161398

Contents

Contributors

Lorena Anderson
State Department of Education
Charleston, West Virginia

Joseph E. Brzeinski
Public Schools
Denver, Colorado

Helen N. Driscoll
Public Schools
Denver, Colorado

Ruth Gagliardo
National Congress of Parents and Teachers

Alma Harrington
State University of New York
Buffalo, New York

Elizabeth Hendryson
National Congress of Parents and Teachers
Albuquerque, New Mexico

Jean Karl
Atheneum Publishers
New York, New York

Lawrence Kasdon
Ferkauf Graduate School
New York, New York

James Kerfoot
Wisconsin State University
River Falls, Wisconsin

Elizabeth Mallory
National Congress of Parents and Teachers

Burley Miller
National Congress of Parents and Teachers
Morgantown, West Virginia

Lee Mountain
University of Houston
Houston, Texas

Carl B. Smith
Indiana University
Bloomington, Indiana

Foreword

THE INTERNATIONAL READING ASSOCIATION'S Perspectives Conferences provide an opportunity to discuss a wide range of significant issues and topics. The conference on "Parents and Reading" was held in connection with IRA's Kansas City Convention. It was jointly sponsored by the National Congress of Parents and Teachers and by IRA and was the first IRA conference concerned specifically with the role of parents and the home in reading instruction.

The conference generated a high degree of interest which is reflected by the papers that are presented here. Furthermore, as a consequence of this conference, the two organizations appointed a joint committee on parents and reading that has continued to be active by presenting programs at IRA conventions and by participating in the PTA Project RISE (Reading Improvement Services Everywhere).

This conference started generating effects before the last talk was completed which is a fitting tribute to its two fine directors, Elizabeth Hendryson and Carl B. Smith.

LEO FAY
Indiana University

The International Reading Association attempts, through its publications, to provide a forum for a wide spectrum of opinion on reading. This policy permits divergent viewpoints without assuming the endorsement of the Association.

You Be the Teacher and I'll Be the Parent

Carl B. Smith

FOR THE CHILD LEARNING TO READ, when is the parent the teacher and the teacher the parent? Parents teach their children many things related to reading, and teachers in school often react to children with parental warmth and encouragement. Parents and teachers are coming together more and more these days with the common goal of trying to improve children's enthusiasm for reading. Parents are frequently in schools as visitors, as curriculum committee members, and as individuals interested in the welfare of their children. One of the reasons for compiling this book was the hope that it would promote intelligent discussion between parent and teacher about reading which would enable them to lead the child to lifelong enjoyment through reading.

None of the articles in this volume were written exclusively for parents even though the title focuses on the parent. The articles also show ways in which teachers and administrators can encourage parents to participate in helping their children learn to read. Just as the parent needs to understand that his child is not the only one in the classroom, the teacher needs to think of ways that the school can work with the parent to make that child grow individually in reading—the goal of both parent and teacher.

In thinking about using reading to promote the business of life, most adults will undoubtedly see more than mechanical decoding skills. Most will associate the nature of the reader with the ability to find material of interest and to read and react critically to what is written. Many believe that the mature reader escapes through reading and finds joy and information to serve him in his own personal way.

1

Reading is indeed one academic tool that humanizes. It is as individual and as personal as walking and talking. Each of us has a distinct voice, and our language reflects our personality. The manner in which we read and the content that we read also reflect the same kind of individuality. Even as we choose from among the chapters in this book, each individual expresses his personal interests and information needs. The conference that spawned these papers was designed to appeal to individuality, and this volume thus reflects a wide variety of ways that parents and teachers can encourage youngsters and can teach them skills that will help them read better.

Hopefully, parents and teachers will view their own adult response to teaching reading with the same flexibility toward encouraging individuality as they do to the learner's individuality. The thoughts presented in this book are in no way meant to prescribe how-to-do-it. They are simply representative samples of ways some parents and teachers have helped their children and have cooperated with the school in providing a more significant reading experience. Each practice should be evaluated, therefore, in light of any new situation. If the suggested activities and ideas found here seem to fit, they are worth a try. If there are circumstances that indicate modifications are in order, then what is described here should be used simply to stimulate new ideas that fit the new situation.

Nowadays the parent is encouraged to assist with learning in whatever way his knowledge or interest suits the learner. The guidelines found in this book should make the reader aware that there are many facets to learning to read and that there are many stages of development through which a child passes on his way to competency and maturity in reading. No one should feel, therefore, that one simple answer or one limited technique will teach every child to read.

Chapters in this book describe how (the home and the general environment contribute language and concepts and thereby condition a child to react favorably or unfavorably toward school and reading) The causes of reading difficulties are discussed to show that causation may involve physical and psychological interferences as well as social and instructional ones. (Interest and motivation play key roles in the energy a child brings to reading and thus should be searched out by the parent and the teacher to take best advantage of the kinds of books that will appeal to the existing drives of the child.)

The book also treats the very practical concerns of the parents' role, how early reading instruction should begin, successful ways some parents have used to teach their children to read, facts about decoding, facts about comprehension, and ways that parents can help with reading instruction in school through the PTA or on their own.

Informed adults can add considerably to the instructional impact of

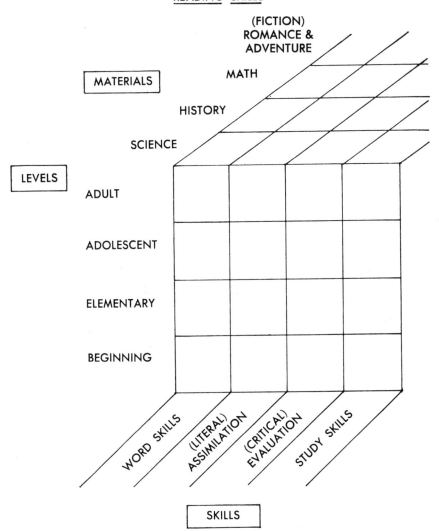

GROUP ANALYSIS CUBE

READING SKILLS

the school program. If one considers the fact that reading depends upon at least three major factors—skills, interests, levels of difficulty—then there is enough work in a class for the teacher and for all the parent help that can be mustered. The possible combinations for any one individual learner are only hinted at in the figure below. But it indicates the value of having many adults concerned and interested in assisting the child with his reading, and it provides a convenient framework to use in analyzing some of the techniques and guides provided in the remainder of this book.

What a Parent Can Do to Help at Home

Ruth Gagliardo

SOME TIME AGO a young mother phoned to ask if she and her husband might call some evening to talk about their daughter's books and reading. "How old is your daughter?" I asked. Back the answer came, "Six months tomorrow—and we don't want to lose any time."

Six months may seem a little young, but childhood is so short a time, especially those golden years before the child is off to school and reading on his own. If in these very early years the child discovers with his parents the everlasting joy of books, his life—whatever its storm and stress—will be forever enriched. For the child to know that his father is having fun when he reads aloud to the family or for the child to see his parents lost in reading books or magazines is a real stimulus when signs and symbols are to be translated into words by the beginning reader.

Goldenson (3) says, "To neglect our children's reading is to miss a golden opportunity to help them toward a fuller life. To take that opportunity, and make the most of it, is to open the door that leads to the most unlimited, the most durable, and the most fruitful of all the sources of enjoyment and enlightenment our world can offer."

That infant of six months had the best start in the world when she was born into a reading family. Already her parents were providing a climate for learning; almost from her birth parents were talking to her, gently, lovingly. The child would hear her mother singing as she moved about her work or her eager father singing nursery rhymes from his own childhood. Before long she would be squirming with delight at "shoe the old

5

horse and shoe the old mare," ending with a clap on baby feet as a grand finale. Dressing would be a delight with her mother's running commentary, often ending with "Now over the head—peek-a-boo!" Adult inflections would begin to appear in the baby's babble. The repertoire of sounds could increase at a surprising rate—and then one day the great breakthrough would come and the first "real" words would be spoken.

Language may grow apace as parents show their pleasure in a child's first speech. Often the child will be heard repeating over and over words whose sounds have special appeal. He chatters endlessly if his environment remains favorable and his hearing is sound. Now experiences must be extended; the child's world must be widened with trips to the fire department, the airport, the railroad station, the market, the zoo. Walks, with daddy if possible, are a delight when taken at the child's pace with frequent stops "to stand and stare." Nature becomes a strong interest, strengthened by the parents' made-up stories of the child and his world, indoors and out.

The public library assumes an importance that will go on for years—one hopes for life. The children's librarian becomes an important person to child and parent. Some books will be borrowed; others suggested by the librarian will be tried out before purchase. Regular family visits to the library are a custom in many families.

Ownership is a necessity if books are to be given right of way, the number of books purchased depending upon the family budget and the generosity of relatives. Hopefully, books are selected with the child's interests and needs in mind. Luckily, too, good children's books are today becoming more readily available in paperbacks with some excellent picture books appearing, such as Marie Etts' *Play with Me* and McCloskey's *Make Way for Ducklings*.

At our house, the most special books of all were homecoming books with the child's name and date marching boldly across the endpaper. The children often helped select these books with much care going into their choosing. At the close of David's sixth homecoming—a family day—he was overheard saying to his younger sister. "Oh, Bettina, aren't you glad we're adopted. Other children have only birthdays, but we have birthdays and homecomings." A happy sigh, and then, "And how I love my ship book. Your day is coming, Bettina. We'll all help you pick the best book of all."

This joy of possession makes the proper care and handling of books easier. And along with care in turning pages come other principles that help when school is attained. A parent's finger running occasionally under a line as a book is read to the child will indicate subtly the left to right reading movements. Quite as easily comes the knowledge that book pages move from front to back while the lines on a single page progress downward. With ABC books the child is likely to identify letters as well as objects; when listening to a favorite book one day, he may demand, "Show me what says 'dog,' Mother; show me." The mother should do this—and without comment.

"Childhood is wrapped clean out of itself with delight, uncritical in its zest," says Walsh (5), writing of childhood reading experiences in *That Eager Zest*. "But the quality of the experience remains," she continues, "above and far beyond the books and the words themselves. Robert P. Tristam Coffin tells how as a little boy he listened to his father's voice saying Shakespeare to him, long before he knew what half the words were about: 'Peter knew from the first, though, that they were something fine. . . . They came up from something deep!' . . . This eagerness of the young child to stand on tiptoe, to reach beyond himself, leads him at last to the wonderful day of discovery: 'I tell you I suddenly read it, Mummy! I read it all by myself.' So a key turns in a lock, and lands of pleasure lie revealed."

Poetry is the great enricher. I want you to hear what Arbuthnot (1) says about it in her exciting new book, *Children's Reading in the Home:*

Fortunately, small children invariably enjoy poetry as long as it is read to them by someone who likes it and reads it well. Their enjoyment comes first from hearing the gay sounds of the words. That is the way people long ago enjoyed the traditional ballads and nursery jingles—from hearing bards . . . sing the old story poems for adults, and nurses or grannies, the jingles for children. The melodies made both kinds of verses fun to hear and so easily remembered that they were passed on by word of mouth for generations. The qualities of the verses that people enjoyed then are the same qualities children first enjoy when they hear poetry today—melody and movement . . . or the "music and the dance of words." So, you see, children discover naturally through their ears what some adults never find out until they read aloud, that poetry, like music, is an aural art. The nursery jingles dance, skip, run, hop, or swing gently. Other poems make a joyful noise or have a solemn quietness. . . . Over and over again, the music and the dance of words, and lines reflect or reinforce the mood or the meaning of a poem from Mother Goose to Browning and Dylan Thomas. Also this movement in words and lines makes little melodies as ear-catching as a song. A child hears you speak the hopping words of Christina Rossetti's

> And timid, funny, brisk little bunny,
> Winks his nose and sits all sunny.

and the tune makes him remember it, so that he begins to say the poem with you. . . . Isn't it better to have children unconsciously memorizing gay, beautiful verse rather than the banal singing commercials, which also utilize melody and movement to make people remember the advertisements in spite of themselves?

A related home activity which is seldom mentioned is the dictated letter in which two- and three-year-olds may participate. Mother may say, "I am writing a letter to Grandma. Would you like to send a letter, too? First, I will write, 'Dear Grandma.' Now you tell me what to say next." Likely as not it will be simply "I love you," but this can be the beginning of a rewarding activity. And how they love to have their letters read back to them, the seed of future written language.

A normally vigorous boy, bedfast for a time, found release from the frustrations of inactivity by dictating to his willing mother long accounts of what he would like to be doing. Illness need not be all on the negative side. This boy read aloud at times to the younger children, while he himself was read to by a proud second grade brother.

Letting the new reader into the family act is all important in encouraging skills—if played lightly. When a beginning reader wishes to share his exciting new (though sometimes still shaky) achievement, adult listener interest should be upon content rather than performance. Home criticism at this point can be a real deterrent to progress. I used to wonder about Linus and that security blanket, but I wondered no more when I learned about the notes his mother put into Linus's school lunch box. "Work hard," they said in effect. "We want to be proud of you."

During the significant early school years we should avoid complications created through overanxious or overambitious parents. These are the years when parent and teacher make a team vital to the child's success and happiness. A fourth grade child was heard to say recently, "My mother and my teacher are friends." What an unbeatable combination that is. Ease of communication is an effective hinge greaser. Conferences such as IRA's annual conventions give parents an understanding of the teacher's task and thus help immeasurably at the local level. The parent's own role will be better understood. What a relief to discover that many of the activities which prepare a child for the great adventure of reading are actually a part of normal everyday living!

Vital to school success is the child's ability to follow instructions. At home he learns to put away his toys, run the vacuum in certain areas, bring in the paper, empty waste baskets and ash trays, dress and undress himself, put his soiled clothing into the hamper, put on and take off outdoor wraps, run errands at home and sometimes in the immediate neighborhood, and make his bed after the age of four (and after a fashion). At home, in the neighborhood, and at nursery school he will learn to play with other children, share certain toys, await his turn, and listen to others. (If only some grown-ups would learn not to interrupt children.) He can telephone, recognize a few simple signs (*stop, men*), distinguish between red and green signs and know their meanings. He may know the hours on the clock when he enters school and what one does before crossing a street. He can use coloring books, paste in his own scrap books, and use blunt scissors. He can assume part of the responsibility of a pet and a bird feeding station, shovel snow, and rake leaves.

And always, given willing parents, he can share books, both imaginative and factual, as his attention span continues to lengthen and his interests widen. Some reading aloud, one hopes, will continue after children are reading independently, sometimes by the child reading aloud and sometimes by a parent.

Luckily there are books to help the parents. Several books might be placed in the PTA collection at school or in the school's professional library to be called to the attention of parents. First, there is Arbuthnot's *Children's Reading in the Home*. One wishes this book could be in every home. The author's knowledge is vast; her enthusiasm is warm and contagious; her annotated book lists for children are reliable and not so extended that choice becomes frustrating. Highly recommended also are *Helping Your Child Improve His Reading (4)* and *Helping Your Child Read Better(3)*. A useful book list, *Let's Read Together,* selected by a special committee of the National Congress of Parents and Teachers and the American Library Association is distributed by both organizations and is now under its third revision. This list has been widely used by parents at home and also as a buying guide by school and public libraries.

The last word is given to Chase (2), who said in *Recipe for a Magic Childhood,* "I know that boys and girls who possess books will live far richer lives than they could otherwise live and will contribute that richness to the communities in which they will become the successful parents of children"—a satisfying goal for any parent or teacher.

REFERENCES

1. Arbuthnot, May Hill. *Children's Reading in the Home.* Scott, Foresman, 1969, 242.
2. Chase, Mary Ellen. *Recipe for a Magic Childhood.* Macmillan, 1967, 20.
3. Goldenson, Robert M. *Helping Your Child to Read Better.* Crowell, 1957, 12.
4. Strang, Ruth. *Helping Your Child Improve His Reading.* Dutton, 1962.
5. Walsh, Frances. *That Eager Zest.* Lippincott, 1961, 9.

The Effect of Environment on Learning to Read

Carl B. Smith

WHILE WORKING with a remedial reading class in Cleveland, I met a young black boy who was ten, in grade four, had failed once, and had great difficulty reading a beginning first grade book. In his regular class he hardly ever talked. Even in the remedial reading class where small groups functioned, he seldom responded and usually gave a *yes* or *no* or a simple shrug of his shoulders in answer to any direct question. After months of prodding, of taking him on visits to supermarkets and museums, we got this boy to begin to talk about himself, to tell us what he did around home. Home to Randy was a slum district with a junk yard one block away. He lived with his mother and two sisters.

What finally got Randy interested in reading was seeing that his own words could be put on paper. He dictated a few sentences about his home, or the policeman, or what he had done over the weekend. His words were typed for him—simple descriptions of familiar scenes, and it took months of effort for Randy to come to the point where he could dictate lines such as these:

The policeman is your friend. He wears a blue suit and hat. He carries a club. When a robber robs a bank, he shoots him. When the robber shoots him, another policeman comes and kills the robber.

Why was a ten-year-old with average intelligence no further along than that? The only thing we were able to ascribe it to was Randy's environment. Hopefully, we caught Randy in time to keep him from landing on the educational slag heap. Hopefully, he has continued to make progress in reading and in other subjects and will be graduated from high school. But many other poor or wealthy children may be condemned by environmental factors to frustration in reading and, therefore, frustration in almost any academic activity.

Children from wealthy families may have reading problems created by the environment. Certain language and reading problems are not isolated to poor neighborhoods. It is not luxury that creates an atmosphere conducive to reading; it is what happens to the child in his home and neighborhood that makes the difference. There is, for example, a community in the United States where almost everyone seems to be wealthy, yet that school system has a reading clinic that is filled to capacity with severe reading problem children. The director of the clinic explains that many children in the community are reared from infancy by nurses. The children may not see their parents for months at a stretch, for the parents are traveling in Europe or working elsewhere while maintaining a permanent residence in this community. If the nurse merely clothes and feeds the child, he can suffer personal deprivation very similar to the child in the slums whose parents are too ignorant or too busy to provide a background for academic achievement.

THE RELATIONSHIP BETWEEN ENVIRONMENT AND READING

Instinctively, most people know that the home and neighborhood have some effect on success in school but do not know specifically what it is that prepares a child for success in reading. For example, is it reading to the child or talking with him? Should parents take him to the zoo or visit the battlefield at Gettysburg? Or should they just place a TV set in his room and let it run 20 hours a day?

To attempt some answers about what things in the environment are related to reading performance, first look at some of the operations involved in reading. The diagram may help to visualize the reading process.

Reading involves the use of language, and language is made up of sounds or words in a system which communicates meaning. A certain facility in the use of this sound system is an understandable prerequisite for reading. But reading is not the sound system; reading is a set of visual symbols that stands for the sound system. Thus, the reader has to be trained to identify and respond to these visual symbols in order to get the message. The reader goes through various operations, several of which evidently are dependent on the environment and the reader's storehouse of experience. The operations in the act of reading might be summarized as follows:

Reading Communication Process*

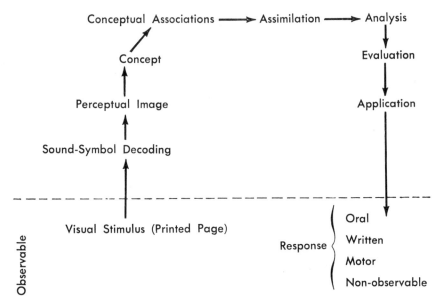

1. *Visual discrimination.* The reader must see the difference between one letter or word and another.
2. *Decoding.* He must translate those visual symbols into the word-sounds that they represent.
3. *Perception.* The reader must recognize the symbol and develop an image; for example, *tree* looks like the one in the backyard.
4. *Concept.* He translates the image into a generalization, for example, maple and oak and evergreen and tall and short.
5. *Association.* The concept must be classified through rapid checking in the memory and be related to past experiences.
6. *Literal comprehension.* A total utterance, a complete passage, is put together, and the unity of the message is recognized by the reader. He can restate it.
7. *Evaluation.* Using logical or experiential criteria, the reader judges the worth of the message.
8. *Synthesis.* With the above data, the reader incorporates the message into a broad scheme of knowledge and experiences for future use.
9. *Application.* The reader decides how to use the message.

The less proficient reader may be able to do only a few of the initial operations, whereas the proficient reader can carry the process through evaluation and synthesis.

How does the environment fit into this scheme? Language is basic.

The average child at school age can understand and manipulate all of the basic sentence structures, and he has a healthy supply of words to work with. His facility with language develops through much listening and responding in the home and in the neighborhood. If a child has not been encouraged early and often to pay attention to language and to imitate language, then he may not have the facility due to a lack of stimulation and practice.

Among the many recent studies of disadvantaged children is a group that shows a correlation between poor language development, poor reading, and a nonverbal environment (Gordon and Wilkerson). A nonverbal environment is one in which the children are not encouraged to speak. They may hear only commands when spoken to and are usually told to keep quiet. The speaking vocabulary of children from a nonverbal environment may consist of only about 500 standard English words compared to about 2,500 words for the child from a verbal environment. His utterances also may be truncated, limited in descriptive power, and hardly recognizable as sentences.

Children must discriminate sounds and visual symbols in order to read. This training towards discriminating sound and shape begins for most children in the crib. The father's voice is different from the mother's. All kinds of bubbling and cooing sounds are aimed at the baby, and the parents are delighted when the baby makes similar sounds in response. The crib has ornaments, a ball, a box, a rag doll, and a mobile. The baby has his attention directed toward these objects and is encouraged to see and feel differences.

Consider the crib—whether poor or rich—where the father and/or the mother do not make noises over the baby, where the baby sees nothing from hour to hour but the sheet and bare walls, and where his only contact comes from a hired nurse or a mother who cannot be bothered with more than feeding and changing him. That kind of deprivation may have long-lasting effects on the reading and the learning performance of the child. There are implications, too, for the effect of sensory stimulation on the decoding operation and on perception. For the eyes and ears must report accurately for decoding and perception to take place.

Concepts. To form a concept or a generalization from the perceptual image, the reader must have a number of experiences with images of a similar nature in order to know, for example, that the image *dog* belongs with the concept *animal.* Usually the parents point out that a *cat* is an animal and a *dog* is an animal and that even though they are different, they are also the same. Most educated parents give these explanations and examples almost without thinking, but they are helping the child to perform abstractions, using language as a tool. Friends and neighbors similarly contribute to the development of concepts.

In school, a child is generally expected to possess a body of concepts concerning the family, the home, the community, animal life, shopping, and the school itself. These are commonly accepted middle-class values, expressed in textbooks in "school talk" which linguists call standard English. The child who lacks these school concepts or who doesn't express concepts in standard English will suffer when he must read about these concepts and try to understand them. An adequate supply of concepts gained from experience and the manipulation of language constitute a basic ingredient for the eventual comprehension of what is read.

Associations. Concepts undergo a rapid-fire interchange with the memory to see what they are related to or associated with. Through associations the reader sets the stage, develops patterns, and sees relationships—all dependent on his previous experience and the arrangement of those concepts in his memory. For example, the phrase "lion in the jungle" may be associated with a trip to the zoo, a jungle movie, a picture book, an African safari, or some kind of street game. Perhaps the phrase does not arouse an association because the supply of experiences does not include "the lion in the jungle." The message, then, has to stumble or stop. Comprehension suffers because the child lacks appropriate items in his memory or experience to handle "the lion in the jungle."

At home the parents can help a child develop a habit of associating and relating things. They can say to the child about "measles," "Do you remember when you had chicken pox? Well, with measles you break out in much the same way." Or they can use riddles: "I am thinking of an animal that has long ears, a fuzzy cottontail, and eats lettuce." Without previous experience, the child cannot solve the riddle or visualize what measles look like. Without the prompting of parents and the stimulation of neighbors who talk about *yesterday* and *tomorrow* and who relate the past to the present and the future—without that kind of stimulation, the child may fail to develop habits of associative thinking. He may remain content to see today's events as single units to remember and may make no attempt to relate them to previous experience or project them into the future.

Literal comprehension. Trying to restate, assimilate, or interpret a passage is what is generally meant by literal comprehension. At home the child is prepared for comprehending a story or a passage through listening to stories and discussing them or by watching TV and retelling the stories. Sometimes, of course, it becomes quite difficult for parents to listen to all the stories the children can talk about. Can't you hear a mother of four little ones crying in anguish as she hears for the fourth time how Underdog saved Sweet Polly from the green monster?

Parents can indeed prepare their children for better comprehension of what they read by asking such questions as "What is it all about? Who are the main characters? What did they try to do? Did they make it?" This series of questions directs the child to take a broader view of the story and leads him away from a mere recall of few facts or incidents. He begins to see a story as a whole with given parts.

Evaluation. A proficient reader makes judgments about the worth of what he is reading. He asks himself: Is it true? Is it logical? Are the conclusions consistent with the data? In school, children are told to read critically and to test what they read against criteria. Certainly some children do train themselves to read critically. But the environment may have a strong influence on the child's development in critical thinking. If his parents and playmates make judgments against evident criteria, the child has a model for critical thinking that will help in evaluating what he reads. On the other hand, in a home where movies, TV, and books are evaluated only on whether "they make me feel good" or are never appraised openly, the child has a model that suggests personal emotion as the primary or only criterion. Parents who praise a movie because it has superior acting or a powerful message for social justice, however, are showing that technical and intellectual criteria are important. They are setting a model of evaluation to guide the child as he reads.

There are other ways in which the environment has subtle yet devastating effects on a child's reading performance. These other influences affect enthusiasm for learning and create negative attitudes toward school and authority.

In a home devoid of books and with an atmosphere lacking in curiosity about the world, life, and government, a child is not likely to develop enthusiasm for learning in school. One of the characteristics of the average failing, disadvantaged child is his lack of enthusiasm for "school" learning. In fact, he often develops negative feelings about learning in school. His parents and playmates may tell him that school learning is a useless or, at most, a very doubtful commodity.

On the other hand, in a home where books are available and are read, where books are read to children, and where the parent talks about the exciting things that go on in school, the child usually looks forward to school.

Concerning the attitudes of disadvantaged children who are failing in school, researchers have found that these children fear or distrust school and the authority that school represents. Either way, they tend to withdraw and fight the school program. It is no wonder, therefore, that many teachers face many students who sulk, dream, or cause trouble. School stands for *them* who are opposed to *us*. *Them* (School) imposes a curriculum, an order, and a language which seem foreign and incomprehensible. In the past, educators have failed to respond to the needs of children. We seem to have said: "I have the gospel, and I will preach it to you. You will listen and answer according to my rules." I think that attitude is changing.

We are not saying that all parents in poverty areas oppose school learning and feel that schools are fearsome. We have growing evidence that people in poverty are acutely interested in the schools and their children's education. Newly organized community groups are getting the neighborhood and the teachers together. It is especially important to join the schools and the parents where the community is impoverished. The teacher usually comes from a middle-class background with its school-oriented language and culture, and often does not know the culture of the black child, the Appalachian child, or the Spanish-American child.

SCHOOL AND COMMUNITY EFFORTS

In order to overcome environmental problems, action from schools and parents is essential. The school has to adjust its curriculum, its teacher attitude, its classroom techniques, and its classroom-school structure and organization. In some cases the school must provide adult education to acquaint the parents with those things that foster school success. Evidently there is no guarantee of success in school no matter what is done at home, but at least parents could know what is related to success in reading.

Some schools and communities have begun programs to get together for the benefit of the children. Let's review some examples of what people are doing to conquer environmental problems that may interfere with success in reading.

1. *Liaison.* Establishing a means of communication is the goal of programs in San Francisco, Cincinnati, and Detroit. Once liaison is established, communication about reading can begin.

Today, removing the barriers of strangeness and fear is part of the principal's job. Ways of accomplishing that goal may range from simple ideas to elaborate plans for better school-community relations.

A Detroit junior high school principal, for instance, cleared out a room and furnished it with comfortable chairs and a large coffee pot. Then he let it be known that the parents, mostly white Appalachian migrants, were welcome. One by one and two by two they are beginning to come, bringing with them their preschool children. The principal takes no advantage of this captive audience; in fact, unless invited, he never goes near their room. But the mothers are gradually losing their fear of the school and are taking opportunities during their visits to talk with the teachers and the principal.

Mothers who have been hired as teachers' aides or teaching assistants turn out to be links with the community. They speak the language or dialect of the community and, whereas their friends might be afraid or embarrassed to ask the teachers or principal questions about the school, they have no misgivings about questioning the aides. Knowing that such interaction takes place challenges the schools to make sure the aides know what is going on and understand any curricular changes that are being instituted.

Many school systems are sending teachers out to work with both preschool and school-age children in the home setting. Actual lessons are taught, with the mothers and brothers and sisters watching and sometimes taking part. The hope is that the mothers will thereby better understand what the schools are trying to do and will also observe and emulate some of the teaching methods.

In Ypsilanti, Michigan, for example, teachers try to involve mothers in the education of their children by showing teaching processes through at-home tutoring. Mothers are also invited to go along on field trips and take part in monthly discussion groups for both fathers and mothers. Early returns show that children who have been involved in the Ypsilanti program outdistance the nonparticipating children in achievement, school motivation, attendance, and relationship with adults.

In Riverton, Wyoming, a part-time social worker familiarizes parents with school learning projects and also supervises a student-to-pupil tutoring program in which junior high school students help elementary school pupils.

In San Francisco, the appointment of a school-community teacher has alleviated many problems. The teacher, acting as a liaison between the school and the parent, shows how the parent can help the child to study and read more effectively and how certain discipline problems can be eased with the help of the home.

2. *Parent education.* Sumter, South Carolina, wants to provide parent education as part of its reading program.

In Sumter, a preprimary project for children of ages three to five is designed to involve parents, staff, and community agencies. The objective is to head off crises before they occur. A preschool checkup is administered by a psychologist who observes and tests the child while his parents are simultaneously interviewed by a social worker. Team members summarize their impressions and later discuss each child's record with a consultant group made up of a project staff member, a local pediatrician, and a child psychiatrist. Parents of children with dependency or immaturity problems are offered immediate family counseling and concrete plans for achieving maturity and independence in the child before he enters school. Children who lack adaptive skills are offered six weeks' pre-education even before Head Start. Children with severe problems are referred to psychiatrists. The project staff makes use of all the community's resources and helps to instigate church programs, neighborhood play groups, family outings, pooled efforts by parents, and the development of new city recreation programs especially aimed at the preschool disadvantaged child.

3. *Building school experiences.* Field trips in Buffalo, Oakland, and St. Louis (which include the parent) offer material for publishing small books for reading about the trip.

The tradition of field trips is especially important for the ghetto child who may never have been more than a few blocks from home. The trips also serve to draw in the parent. Often parents not only accompany the children but are included in the planning. In St. Louis, a direct appeal is made to parents. The principals invite the parents to school where their cooperation in helping the child learn to read is enlisted. They are told of the relationship between education and the kinds of jobs their children might be able to hold. This information is reinforced by field trips where the children see people at work and begin to understand the relationship between what they do in school and what kind of lives they can lead.

Using the field trip as a widening experience, the skilled teacher can capitalize on it, both before and after, through discussions, experience charts, new word lists, map making of the route covered, written reports, compositions, poems about the experience, thank you notes to the hosts, and other activities that incorporate language arts skills.

4. *Interaction and discussion.* Community and volunteer tutors are used in Indianapolis, New York City, Cincinnati, and Montebello.

In New York City, ten-year-olds tutor seven-year-olds. It is part of a Hunter College tutoring program involving thirty of the college's prospective teachers and 62 fifth and sixth graders from PS 158. The college juniors tutor the youngsters who, in turn, tutor second and third graders. The fifth and sixth graders get help with their own learning problems from the college students, then reinforce what they learn by helping younger children who have similar difficulties. An unlooked-for advantage is that the older students have gained new respect for themselves and for their classroom teachers.

The National School Volunteer Program is well known. It began in New York City and has spread to most of the major cities. Women volunteers are assigned to one school for at least three half-days a week during the school year to serve as individual tutors. Although the school volunteers have no figures to show reading improvement, administrators have had loud praise for their efforts. Besides giving the children individual, undivided attention, these tutors are able to discover little situations that can be of great help to the classroom teacher. For instance, simply finding out that a little girl of eight stays up half the night watching the late show can explain her lack of attention in class and lead to some efforts to convince her mother of the value of sleep.

In the Two Bridges area of New York City, between Brooklyn and Manhattan bridges on the lower East Side, 21 mothers have been hired as reading assistants for four hours a day, five days a week. In general, the project achieved what it set out to do: to help children retarded in reading to catch up, not only with the average readers but with the best in the class. The intangible benefits of giving the children individual attention, helping improve self-images by seeing their own parents on the school staff in a respected position, providing 21 new links with an impoverished area of the city, and demonstrating that undereducated parents can help solve one of the schools' major problems actually proved as vital as the help that was given the children in reading. The Two Bridges reading assistants received one week of training and continuing observation and inservice training throughout the year (although the latter was rather hit or miss), depending on the available time of the training supervisor and the teachers to whom the assistants were assigned.

There are many variations in the use of tutors, but one of the most closely structured programs is the one in Indianapolis. It illustrates both the advantages of a carefully planned program and the use of nonprofessionals drawn from the immediate neighborhood of the school.

Since the program began, many Indianapolis children who were not expected to read at the end of first grade are reading and reading well. Called "programed tutoring" and scientifically designed, it is saving poor-risk first graders from failure and turning them into average readers. It has been so successful that the Ford Foundation has given a grant to extend it to those children who seem to have the least chance for success.

The program uses neighborhood tutors with no special training for teaching except that given in the program itself. The use of nonprofessionals not only saves money but the children respond to people who can speak their own language and understand their problems, perhaps first hand.

The difference between programed tutoring and the normal one-to-one tutoring is that programed tutoring carefully structures the behavior of the tutor who is told how to act and what to say. She follows precise written instructions in dealing with the children. In five steps, the tutor leads each child through his reading lesson, using the questions and directions that have been written for that specific lesson.

5. *Book distribution.* A book club gives a child a free book for his own after he shows that he has read four from the classroom library.

Sometimes fresh ideas spring from summer projects. In St. Louis, students in 76 classrooms were encouraged to read by being given books as prizes. To get his first book, a student needed only to show that he had a public library card. Then he could earn up to nine books, getting one for every two he read outside of class. The program cost only $4,000 to initiate, and the state education department provided the money under Title I funding for library books. So many of the pupils earned the maximum number of books that the schools were compelled to seek more money from the state. The parents also became involved. More than one father built a bookshelf for his child, sometimes the first bookshelf the home had known. Some mothers, for the first time, got library cards for themselves. Among the students, many poor readers became avid readers. Homes with books encourage reading.

6. *Language development.* Kansas City, Missouri, encouraged community participation by turning an elementary school auditorium into a first-class professional theatre with a professional director and local theater group putting on plays for the children. Vocabulary and reading activities accompanied each performance.

7. *Sensitivity training for teachers and parents.* San Bernardino, California, has a six-month program of biweekly meetings involving poverty parents and teachers who meet to break down emotional barriers and reach an understanding of the child's environment. These are just a few examples of programs to counteract environmental effects on reading. These programs are described in *Reading Problems and the Environment,* published by IRA in 1969.

What Does it All Mean?

In this presentation we have summarized the research on environment, looked at aspects of the environment that relate to operations in the reading process, and described some programs whose intent it is to overcome the environment.

Research indicates that the following environmental factors are often related to poor reading:

- Inadequate vocabulary—even in a nonstandard dialect.
- Lack of early experience with a variety of shapes and sounds.
- Few experiences (concepts) that relate to the content of the books used in school.
- Lack of stimulation through books.
- Lack of discussion, questions and answers, cause and effect conversations —"tell me all about it."
- Negative attitudes toward school and authority and learning.
- Rigid restrictions on children's behavior.

The school and the community must work together to set up programs to identify and change environmental problems. Here is a suggested procedure for a school and community (parent) committee to use in setting up programs to overcome the parts of the environment that interfere with reading.

1. *Survey the Needs Related to Reading*

What factors in the neighborhood may interfere with the reading performance of some, or even all, of the children? Consider, for example, poor self-image, lack of language stimulation, nonstandard dialect, and negative attitude toward school and authority. Use study committees, questionnaires, and school records.

2. *Assess Resources*

What people, facilities, money, and procedures can you use to act on the needs? Try interested teachers and community groups, temporary buildings, contingency funds and federal grants, and participation in pilot programs.

3. *Consider Possible Solutions—Programs*

What do research, demonstration programs, and common sense suggest as ways that will ease the reading problems associated with the environment? Consider ungraded classes, home-school teachers, family library programs, tutors, directed field trips, and stimulating materials.

4. *Include the Community in Planning and in Execution*

What groups or individuals should help solve some of the reading problems? Consider the PTA, local business associations, political pressure groups, professional associations, and interested parents. These people are important not only for generating good will but also for selling the programs to the community and for finding resources to operate the proposed programs.

5. *Set Specific Objectives*

What should the children (or adults) be able to do as a result of your program? With a home-school coordinator program, for example, the child and the parent should be able to conduct a simple reading and comprehension exercise after a visit from the coordinator. (Establishing specific objectives becomes important in "selling" the program to others and in evaluating its effectiveness.)

6. *Clarify Operational Procedures*

Who are the people with responsibility and what are the rules for the programs? Publicize the leader of the program and the guidelines for its operation. A necessary condition is that the principal must give the program leader freedom to operate. Innovative programs, like innovative teachers, must be free to make mistakes or it is unlikely that anything exciting can happen.

7. *Submit a Proposal*

If the program needs central approval for any reason, write a proposal that describes the first six steps and gives a budget.

8. *Evaluate the Program*

Are the procedures being carried out? Have the objectives been realized to some degree? Be willing to evaluate in terms of the response of the teaching staff, the pupils, and the local community.

CONCLUSION

We parents and teachers have too much at stake as individuals and as a society to ignore the problems of the environment that interfere with school success. Researchers, teachers, and parents have made some exemplary first steps in the programs described earlier. What we need to do now is grab hold of similar programs and make our schools places where all children can learn and where the community stands taller and prouder because of the education provided there.

Causes of Reading Difficulties

Lawrence M. Kasdon

As we examine the literature concerning causes of reading difficulties, we can identify with the six blind men who described the elephant. Just as they could not agree, offering six very different descriptions, so researchers from the same or different disciplines offer varying and sometimes conflicting explanations of the causes of reading difficulties. Indeed, sometimes it seems as if we have had a corneal transplant only to discover that the cause of the blindness is not the clouded cornea. Instead, it is a lesion in the brain that not only interferes with sight but also with reason.

Let us explore our mythical elephant, however, remembering our blindness and hoping that the lesion does not affect our thinking processes. The blind men in the poem were fortunate because they knew that they were trying to describe a single animal, an elephant. Those of us who work in the area of remedial reading sometimes feel as if we are as blind and confused as the wise men in the poems as far as our state of knowledge goes. Many of us believe that we are attempting to deal with an entire menagerie and yet there are many dedicated investigators who insist we are only dealing with an elephant.

DIRECT CAUSES ARE DIFFICULT TO IDENTIFY

What confounds our problem even more is that the experts who write about reading may specialize in ophthalmology, pediatrics, neurology, linguistics, psychology, education, or literature. A Tower of Babel exists about terminology. One wonders if people speaking and writing about reading difficulties are really communicating. In commenting on this situation, Harris (*14*) writes:

> Thus a child may be labeled a case of reading disability or deficiency, a retarded reader, an underachiever in reading, a case of specific language disability, or perceptually handicapped. The one common element among these terms is the agreement that the pupil's progress in reading is unsatisfactory in terms of his potential. Beyond this, there is wide disagreement not only regarding terminology but also on the significance of various etiological factors and on the appropriateness and efficacy of different methods of treatment.

Thus, we cannot even enjoy playing the great American game of labeling something, thereby thinking that we know what that something is.

I agree that there is no one label that is appropriate for all individuals whose reading progress is unsatisfactory in terms of their potential. At the risk of contradicting myself, I shall, in this paper, refer to such individuals as underachievers in reading, regardless of what other problems they may or may not have.

In one of the better known attempts at categorizing remedial reading cases, Rabinovitch (*20*) suggests three major categories that have grown out of his diagnostic studies:

1. *Primary reading retardation*—cases in which the cause is biological with no brain damage. "The defect is in the ability to deal with letters and words as symbols, with resultant diminished ability to integrate the meaningfulness of written material. The problem appears to reflect a basic disturbed pattern of neurological organization."

2. *Secondary reading retardation*—the child possesses normal capacity to learn but this capacity has been vitiated by such external factors as emotional blocking, psychoses, and limited opportunity for schooling.

3. *Brain injury with reading retardation*—"Capacity to learn to read is impaired by frank brain damage manifested by clear-cut neurological deficits."

These categories appear to be clear-cut and, at first, we feel we can at last classify our reading underachievers into neat categories. Rabinovitch continues, however, "It is more difficult to be certain into which group a particular case fits than it is to recognize that there are three groups."

Perhaps causes of underachievement in reading were best described over twenty years ago by Helen Robinson (*24*). She attempted to identify and measure the various causal factors in a group of 22 severely retarded readers. Designating herself as psychologist and reading technician, Robinson obtained the help of a social worker, a psychiatrist, a pediatrician, a neurologist, an endocrinologist, and a reading specialist. She concluded an anomaly was causal if improvement in reading resulted upon correction or use of appropriate compensations. Robinson found that maladjusted homes or poor interfamily relationships were contributing causes in 54.5 percent of the cases. Visual anomalies were found in 73 percent of the 22 cases but were considered causes of reading failure in only 50 percent of these cases. There were significant emotional problems in 41 percent of the 22 cases studied, with 22 percent causal. Inappropriate teaching methods appeared to be the cause of reading failure in 18 percent of the 22 cases.

Alexia (word blindness) or some other neurological problem was considered a cause of reading failure in 18 percent of the cases. Because of the current interest in neurology and reading it is interesting to note what Robinson wrote in 1946:

> The present study shows that many pupils who had made little or no progress in learning to read before this diagnostic study were not victims of alexia in the judgment of the neurologists. Moreover, a few cases diagnosed as alexia made progress beyond the level expected of a child with such a handicap.

Speech and functional auditory factors were found to be contributing causes of reading disability in 18 percent of the 22 cases; dyslalia (an articulatory defect) was considered a cause in 14 percent.

Robinson concluded that those most seriously retarded in reading evidenced the greatest number of anomalies, whereas the least retarded presented the fewest number. Another important conclusion made in this study was that when a group of specialists tried to evaluate the anomalies for each subject, certain of the anomalies had no direct relationship to the reading problem. Furthermore, there was not complete agreement among Robinson's experts as to which factors caused reading retardation. Today there is still lack of agreement.

Robinson's study provides many valuable clues, but because of her small sample and her research design, her results must be regarded as tentative. It is most unfortunate that someone has not done a follow-up study. However, the disagreement concerning the potency of various causes reported in the findings of Robinson's study has been reinforced by different investigators. Such disagreements may stem from the research design used by the various investigators as well as from the nature of the population studied. Other factors that might account for differences in findings are teaching methods and socioeconomic status. Disagreement may also be partly due to the use of different tests and to varying norms. For example, in Robinson's study the ophthalmologist considered hyperopia (far-sightedness) of less than $+1.50$ diopters as not needing correction, whereas Eames (*10*) maintained that hyperopia between +0.50 to +1.50 diopters needed correction.

There are still methodological research problems in attempting to establish causality even when the criteria of replication and valid instrumentation are met. First, there is Robinson's finding that those most retarded in reading evidenced the greatest number of anomalies. Even if we thought we knew all of the causes of reading failure, these causes rarely occur in isolation; consequently, we get an interaction effect. For example, if a child has emotional problems, suffers from binocular incoordination, and was brain damaged at birth, all of these in combination may be a greater handicap in learning to read than if any one occurred singly. Second, with our present state of knowledge we are not certain we can measure some of these anomalies. Maybe the brain damage can account for the emotional problem, or was the emotional problem caused by reading failure? Perhaps there has been a self-remission of the brain damage, but the child still behaves as if he were brain damaged. His condition may be further aggravated by the fact that his first grade teacher excused herself from trying to teach him to read because he was such an obnoxious little brat with a damaged brain and, you know, no one can be expected to teach such a child anything.

How many etiological factors do we have operative? How much are they interacting to produce different effects than any one would have by itself? Would the teacher have tried to teach the child to read if he had not been obnoxious, although still brain damaged? Would she have been able to use the appropriate methodology? We cannot answer these questions.

When we attempt to get at causes of retardation in reading, we typically study subjects between nine and twenty years of age who already evidence difficulties in reading. Since we work from the effect and try to find the causes, this type of research is known as ex post facto research. Ex post facto research has severe limitations for the generation of explanations. Because of these limitations, we can expect that utilization of this methodology to determine causes of reading difficulty would result in disagreement and contradictions. [For a more complete discussion of ex post facto research see Kerlinger (*18*).]

SOME PHYSICAL FACTORS

Parents are doubtlessly curious about childbirth and reading. Probably the most comprehensive study on this point was made by Kawi and Pasamanick (*17*). These two researchers found that the following conditions differentiated a group of underachievers in reading from so-called normals: premature births, toxemias of pregnancy (preeclampsia, hypertensive disease), and bleeding during pregnancy (before third trimester, placenta praevia, premature separation of the placenta).

Let us examine the effects of visual defects on reading. In a number of studies, farsightedness, astigmatism, binocular incoordination, and fusion difficulties have been reported as having a negative effect on reading achievement (23, 26). Parents have a false sense of security when they rely on the Snellen Vision Test, typically administered in most schools. While it is useful as a screening device for truck drivers, it is not useful in screening visual defects that may interfere with reading. The Snellen eye chart primarily identifies people who are nearsighted. As a matter of fact, nearsighted pupils tend to be better readers than those who are farsighted (27). Also, vision examiners often miss identifying important visual handicaps by testing at 20 feet rather than at the reading distance. Visual acuity at a reading distance is often different from far point visual acuity (11).

Another of the fictions about vision is that kindergarteners' eyes are too immature for them to start to learn to read. Eames (11) found children at five years of age had more accommodative power than at any subsequent age. The poorest near visual acuity found among the pupils studies was quite sufficient for reading the usual texts. It must be for reasons other than vision that reading should not be taught in kindergarten.

Research findings and conclusions on the relationship of specific visual anomalies to reading disability are contradictory. Some of these contradictions may be explained in part in terms of the ability of the child to compensate for the defect; or they may be explained in terms of his age or emotional makeup; or these contradictions may indicate a central dysfunction which is reflected in the motor responses.

> Visual factors may be directly related, contributory, or coincidental to the reading disability. The relationship of patterns of visual defects to visual perception and to specific reading disabilities needs to be studied further (27).

Poor hearing, while relatively infrequent in reading disabilities, may be very important when it occurs. There is some evidence that children with high-frequency hearing losses tend to fail in the primary grades (16). A large proportion of the consonant sounds, such as *p, s, t, b, k, v, c, fl, s, th,* are found among the high tones (25).

Auditory acuity, auditory memory, and auditory discrimination are all necessary for progress in word recognition (29). Walters and Kosowski (28) indicate that unless retarded readers are highly motivated, they may pay less attention to reading because auditory discrimination requires so much effort on their part. We can say with some assurance that reading underachievers frequently show marked deficiencies in auditory discrimination; consequently, giving them a heavy dose of phonics in the beginning stages of remediation may in certain cases aggravate the situation.

Endocrine gland defects and deficiencies are less common among underachievers in reading but, when present, create severe problems if left untreated. Eames (*11*) reports that the majority of his reading cases with endocrine problems are of the especially mild to moderate *hypothyroid* type, which had been undetected for some time.

The debilitating effects of chronic poor health require careful evaluation. Malnutrition, asthma, and rheumatic fever may be involved with reading problems. Any condition resulting in lowered energy may interfere with concentration and effort in learning to read (*15*).

INTELLECTUAL FACTORS

One way to avoid teaching children to read is to decide that the children are stupid. Most of the group intelligence tests administered beyond third grade require the pupil to do some reading. However, if a child cannot read the test, he will get a low score, particularly on any part that is verbal (*19*). If the child's reading does not improve, he will continue to do poorly on group intelligence tests, in terms of his own ability, as he advances through the grades. School teachers or counselors may fail to realize that a mediocre verbal score on a group intelligence test might be influenced by poor reading achievement. If this is the case, the pupil may be counseled out of aspiring to go to college.

Two years ago twin brothers were brought to our reading clinic because they were not doing as well as their peers at a well-known suburban high school. Their older brother and sister were always honor pupils, but somehow the twins were never able to do top-notch academic work. The records from their school showed their IQs to be at the low end of the normal range on a group intelligence test. The school counselor had recommended the twins be prepared for a trade. However, when an individual intelligence test was administered to them, they scored at the 99th percentile. After informing the twins, their mother, and the school counselor of our findings, we began remediation. Within one semester they were functioning well above grade level in reading and study skills. As part of the study skills instruction we taught them how to beat the system. The following year they were placed in the top section of the academic track.

Learning Modality Problems

A question frequently asked is "Are there some children who are more hand minded than eye minded?" The answer is "yes." The corollary question usually is "Are such children stupid?" The answer within the context of remedial reading is "no." A substantial number of children seen at reading clinics have convinced themselves through repeated failure in learning to read that they are dumber than their peers. Sometimes this self-concept is fostered by parents and teachers. In a sound remedial procedure one of the first things the clinician must do is convince the student that he can learn to read. In some instances, the clinician has a difficult time convincing the student that he is not stupid.

Emotional Factors

Parent groups frequently ask whether some children have a "mental block" toward learning to read. I suppose most of us have mental blocks toward things that we do not do well. In addition, there may be other dynamics at work that my colleagues in psychiatry could supply. It may be that some children use failing to learn to read as an attention-getting device. Have you ever heard some teachers express concern about a child who is not learning to read? Most teachers are quite dedicated, and I am sure that at the beginning of each school year practically every elementary school teacher in the United States vows that she will bring every child in her classroom up to grade level in reading by the end of the year.

I might also say that it is not atypical of middle class parents to discuss little Johnny's reading problems in not so *sotto voce*. To help things along, Johnny is compared with a successful sister in the not-so-ego-building process.

Many parents try to help their underachievers in reading. My experience from hundreds of conferences with parents is that such help usually results in upsetting both the child and the parent. I am sure that if the child did not already have a block toward reading, one would develop after a few evening sessions of tears and screaming. I become concerned about the guilt and even hostility toward the child that results from such encounters. My advice to parents is not to try to tutor their children unless both parties are comfortable in the situation.

Related to the mental block question is the following: Do underachievers in reading display other types of emotional problems and are these emotional problems the cause of their not doing well in reading? I would say that most of the cases I have seen do have emotional problems about their reading. Parents and society put enormous pressures on the child to learn to read. As the child progresses through the grades, he is likely to become more and more frustrated if he cannot read assignments. The cases that cause me more concern are those who are not upset about their reading. For the most part, these are the ones that have given up; and I know that if they really feel that way, I am going to have a difficult time teaching them to read.

As far as the causal relationship between reading and emotional problems is concerned, there seems to be no conclusive research to answer the question of which comes first. This is not to say that this aspect of diagnosis has been neglected. Almost everyone who writes on the subject offers a different list of presenting symptoms and a different explanation of their psychodynamics. Nevertheless, in reading clinics across the United States clients with emotional problems are being helped to learn to read. If the emotional problems interfere or are still severe at the conclusion of reading therapy, usually the clinician will recommend mental health therapy for the child.

I would estimate that about 85 percent of the children of normal intelligence can learn to read by almost any reading method currently in use in the schools. The remainder will have difficulty in learning to read. One factor causing such difficulty may be that these children have specific styles of learning to read which evidently were not used with them. One aspect of a diagnosis is to discover how the child can learn; this factor is particularly true with severely retarded readers or nonreaders. Among these, there are some who learn best with their hands—that is, using their fingers to trace words while saying them. This method is called the Fernald Kinesthetic technique. Other extreme examples might be visual or auditory learners. If the child is only a visual learner, teaching him phonics will probably compound his problems. If the child is an auditory learner, phonics will be an essential method for him.

EDUCATIONAL FACTORS

Another popular fallacy is that there would not be any reading problems if the schools would quit using the sight method and teach the children phonics. First of all, I know of no public schools in five states in which I have worked where phonics is not being taught. Of course, this does not meet the issue as raised, for the phonics proponents believe that we should begin reading instruction with phonics. I do not agree that reading should be restricted to figuring out the pronunciation of words to the neglect of such reading skills as comprehension. I do agree, however, that more phonics should be—and could be—taught systematically in the first grade in order to make children independent readers earlier. Unfortunately, the authors of many reading textbooks were influenced by research conducted in 1937 (9) in which investigators found that children whose mental ages were below seven years of age were able to do little or nothing on a phonics test. This point of view prevailed despite Gates' research (12) in which he sensibly reasoned that the child's reading progress is not dependent solely on his mental ability. He concluded that such things as the specific method and materials and the speed with which pupils are required to move along all influence the progress of the child.

More recently we have evidence from the First Grade Studies (3) supporting my point of view regarding the teaching of phonics, plus expressing other important points: "There is no one method that is so outstanding that it should be used to the exclusion of others." The First Grade Studies concluded that there was greater difference in pupil achievement among teachers using the same method than there was between methods. In other words, the teacher and the school make the difference in how much the children achieve in reading rather than the specific methods examined in the First Grade Studies.

DYSLEXIA, PERCEPTUAL HANDICAPS, MINIMUM BRAIN DAMAGE, AND OTHER FASHIONABLE TERMS

On February 20, 1969, an article appeared in the *New York Times* with the heading, "Scientists Assay Dyslexia Clues. Origins of Reading Disorder Are Sought by Committee." Below are extracts from the article:

Dyslexia, a catch-all term for numerous reading disorders in children, continues to perplex parents, physicians, and educators who are trying, with little success, to learn why Johnnys can't read. About one in seven school-age children in the United States suffers some kind of malfunction, Dr. Charles A. Ullman, a psychologist, said early this week. Dr. Ullman . . . is executive director of the National Advisory Committee on Dyslexic and Related Reading Disabilities.

In the past, most experts guessed that about 15 percent of all children in the nation could not learn to read because of fundamental malfunctions in either their physical or emotional makeup.

Now, five freshly completed studies corroborate that estimate, Dr. Ullman said. After six months of discussion, there is still one hurdle the experts have not been able to overcome—how to define dyslexia. The psychologist, the neurologist, the educator, the audiologist, and the opthalmologist (sic) all view dyslexia from different grandstands.

A few points, however, the experts do agree on: dyslexia is not a disease in the pathological sense; it does not mean a child is emotionally disturbed; it does not mean his education has been inferior; and it does not mean the child necessarily has a learning problem.

I can understand how the various investigators participating in this study might obtain divergent figures as to the incidence of dyslexia. As I have indicated in my discussion of learning modalities, the student's education may not have been inferior, but his teacher may have been unable to identify his particular style of learning to read. I fail to comprehend why the committee agreed that the child does not have a learning problem. If a child is a nonreader or is severely retarded in reading, I believe that he definitely has a learning problem and is usually emotionally disturbed about it to some degree.

Let us continue with the last paragraph of the article, as it summarizes the confusion among the various writers on dyslexia.

The fundamental causes of dyslexia also are obscure. Some guess a genetic factor may be involved while others look to neurological, psychological, physiological, or socioeconomic reasons.

In an outstanding collection of readings on dyslexia, Cruickshank (4) points out the confusion about defining dyslexia:

If a child diagnosed as dyslexic in Philadelphia moved to Bucks County, 10 miles north, he would be called a child with a language disorder. In Montgomery County, Maryland, a few miles south, he would be called a child with special or specific reading problems. In Michigan, he would be called a child with perceptual disturbances. In California, he would be called either a child with educational handicaps or a neurologically handicapped child. In Florida or New York State, he would be called a brain-injured child. In Colorado, the child would be classified as having minimal brain dysfunction.

Since 1955 forty-three different terms, generally referring to the dyslexic child, have appeared in the literature. Fortunately, although the name for the disorder may change, the child remains the same. . . .

I am inclined to agree with Harris (14) that *dyslexia* is a term used primarily by medical specialists to define a subgroup within the group referred to by the term *reading disability*.

One of the questions frequently raised in connection with dyslexia is, "If my child is left-handed or hasn't developed a consistent choice of hands, how will this affect his reading?" All I can say in answer to the question is that I doubt that it will affect his reading. Some investigators agree with Zangwill (*30*) "that an appreciable proportion of dyslexic children show poorly developed laterality and that in these there is commonly evidence of slow speech development. . . ." Even Zangwill speculated as to why some poorly lateralized children learn to read well. Such writers as Balow (*1*) fail to find any relationship between laterality and poor reading, a conclusion based on a survey of an unselected population. Benton (*2*) expresses some doubt about the relationship of directional sense and expressed the opinion that when it does exist, it may be related to age, intelligence, or other syndromes. In a summary of research, Zeman (1967) cited only three studies out of fourteen that reported significant relationships between laterality and reading.

Parent groups frequently ask about some new method of diagnosis and treatment of remedial reading that has been reported in the popular press. Let me briefly mention one that has attracted a great deal of attention. Delacato (*6, 7, 8*) emphasizes the attainment of developmental stages in neurological maturity resulting in cerebral dominance. In his second book (*7*), Delacato elaborated on his theory of neurological organization and advocated the importance of creeping and stylized walking activities for the development of dominance and the prevention of language disorders.

In a criticism of Delacato's theory, Glass and Robbins (*13*) analyzed fifteen studies offered by Delacato in his three books as support for his theory. Without exception, the studies cited by Delacato as a "scientific appraisal" of his theory of neurological organization were demonstrated to be of dubious value. Two studies evaluating this theory were conducted by Robbins (*21, 22*). Neither of Robbins' studies supported Delacato's theories, either with second grade pupils or with retarded readers.

CONCLUSIONS

I have presented some of the facts and fiction concerning causes of reading difficulties, including my own point of view. Because of space limitations, I have not discussed some other important topics related to suspected causes of reading difficulties. These shall have to await another paper.

As we have seen, there are many causes of underachievement in reading which interact with one another so that it is extremely difficult to isolate them and determine which is the cause and which the effect. Instead of engaging in ex post facto studies, we need to carefully design longitudinal studies such as deHirsch's (*5*) before we shall be able to speak with certainty about causes of reading failure. Such longitudinal studies will be most profitable if they are conducted by an interdisciplinary team. From what we now know, such research will require more expertise than any one individual can provide.

Whether we are engaged in research or in remediating reading problems, we must be careful about pinning labels on a child. Such labels sometimes become self-fulfilling prophecies and in themselves do not solve reading difficulties. At our clinic at the Ferkauf Graduate School we have clients referred to us from hospitals, social agencies, and other reading clinics and schools. The clients come with all sorts of labels, such as specific dyslexia, perceptually handicapped, alexia, autistic, and what have you. As mentioned previously, labels often do not communicate usable information. Regardless of such labels, we have to find out what it will take to teach the individual to read and get on with the job. We may not cure his "dyslexia," but we do teach him to read.

We should never become smug about what we know concerning the causes of reading difficulties. In the inexorable advance of science, today's fact may become tomorrow's fiction.

REFERENCES

1. Balow, Irving H. "Lateral Dominance of Characteristics and Reading Achievement in First Grade," *Journal of Psychology*, 55 (1963), 323-328.
2. Benton, Arthur L. "Dyslexia in Relation to Form Perception and Directional Sense," in John Money (Ed.), *Reading Disability: Progress and Research Needs in Dyslexia.* Baltimore: Johns Hopkins Press, 1962, 81-102.
3. Bond, Guy L. "First Grade Studies: An Overview," *Elementary English*, 43 (1966), 465.
4. Cruickshank, William M. "The Problem of Delayed Recognition and Its Correction," in Arthur H. Keeney and Virginia T. Keeney (Eds.), *Dyslexia: Diagnosis and Treatment of Reading Disorders.* St. Louis: C. V. Mosby, 1968, 84.
5. deHirsch, Katrina, J. J. Jansky, and W. S. Langford. *Predicting Reading Failure: A Preliminary Study.* New York: Harper and Row, 1966.
6. Delacato, C. H. *The Treatment and Prevention of Reading Problems.* Springfield, Illinois: Charles C. Thomas, 1959.
7. Delacato, C. H. *The Diagnosis and Treatment of Speech and Reading Problems.* Springfield, Illinois: Charles C. Thomas, 1963.
8. Delacato, C. H. *Neurological Organization and Reading.* Springfield, Illinois: Charles C. Thomas, 1966.
9. Dolch, E. W., and M. Bloomster. "Phonics Readiness," *Elementary School Journal*, 38 (1937), 201-205; as quoted in A. J. Harris *How to Increase Reading Ability* (4th ed.). New York: Longmans, Greene, 1961, 328.
10. Eames, Thomas H. "The Ocular Conditions of 350 Poor Readers," *Journal of Educational Research*, 32 (September 1938), 10-13.

11. Eames, Thomas H. "Physical Factors in Reading," *Reading Teacher*, 15 (May 1962), 427-432.

12. Gates, A. I. "The Necessary Age for Beginning Reading," *Elementary School Journal*, 37 (1937), 497-508.

13. Glass, Gene V., and Melvyn P. Robbins. "A Critique of Experiments on the Role of Neurological Organization in Reading Performance," *Reading Research Quarterly*, 3 (1967), 5-51.

14. Harris, Albert J. "Diagnosis and Remedial Instruction in Reading," *Innovation and Change in Reading Instruction*, Sixty-seventh Yearbook of the National Society for the Study of Education, Part II. Chicago, Illinois: University of Chicago Press, 1968, 159-161, 169.

15. Harris, Albert J., and Florence Roswell. "Clinical Diagnosis of Reading Disability," *Journal of Psychology*, 36 (1953), 323-340.

16. Henry, Sybil. "Children's Audiograms in Relation to Reading Achievement," *Pedagogical Seminary and the Journal of Genetic Psychology*, 70 and 71 (June and September 1947), 211-231, 3-48, 49-63.

17. Kawi, Ali A., and Benjamin Pasamanick. "Prenatal and Paranatal Factors in the Development of Childhood Reading Disorders," *Monographs of the Society for Research in Child Development*, 24 (1959), 2-80.

18. Kerlinger, Fred N. *Foundations of Behavioral Research*. New York: Holt, Reinhart and Winston, 1965.

19. McLaulin, J. C., and G. B. Schiffman. "A Study of the Relationship between the California Test of Mental Maturity and the WISC Test for Retarded Readers," mimeographed manuscript, as quoted in Gilbert Schiffman, "Dyslexia as an Educational Phenomenon: Its Recognition and Treatment," in John Money (Ed.), *Reading Disability*. Baltimore: Johns Hopkins Press, 1962.

20. Rabinovitch, Ralph D. "Dyslexia: Psychiatric Considerations," in John Money (Ed.), *Reading Disability*. Baltimore: Johns Hopkins Press, 1962.

21. Robbins, Melvyn P. "Delacato Interpretation of Neurological Organization," *Reading Research Quarterly*, 1 (1966), 57-78.

22. Robbins, Melvyn P. "Influence of Special Programs on the Development of Mental Age and Reading," Cooperative Research Project No. S-349, U. S. Department of Health, Education and Welfare, Office of Education, 1965; as quoted in Albert J. Harris, "Diagnosis and Remedial Reading," *Innovations and Change in Reading Instruction*, Sixty-seventh Yearbook of the National Society for the Study of Education, Part II. Chicago: University of Chicago Press, 1968.

23. Robinson, H. M. "Visual Efficiency and Reading Status in the Elementary School," in H. M. Robinson and H. K. Smith (Eds.), *Clinical Studies in Reading, III*, Educational Monographs No. 97. Chicago: University of Chicago, 1968.

24. Robinson, Helen M. *Why Pupils Fail in Reading*. Chicago: University of Chicago Press, 1946.

25. Spache, George D. *Toward Better Reading*. Champaign, Illinois: Garrard, 1963, 113.

26. Spache, George D., and C. E. Tillman. "A Comparison of the Visual Profiles of Retarded and Non-Retarded Readers," *Journal of Developmental Reading*, 5 (1962), 101-108.
27. Strang, Ruth. *Reading Diagnosis and Remediation,* IRA Research Fund Monograph. Newark, Delaware: International Reading Association, 1968, 20.
28. Walter, R. H., and Irene Kosowski. "Symbolic Learning and Reading Retardation," *Journal of Consulting Psychology*, 27 (1963), 75-82.
29. Wepman, Joseph M. "Auditory Discrimination, Speech and Reading," *Elementary School Journal*, 60 (1960), 325-333.
30. Zangwill, O. L. "Dyslexia in Relation to Cerebral Dominance," in John Money (Ed.), *Reading Disability: Progress and Research Needs in Dyslexia*. Baltimore: Johns Hopkins Press, 1962, 111.
31. Zeman, Samuel Steve. "A Summary of Research Concerning Laterality and Reading," *Journal of the Reading Specialist*, 6 (1967), 116-123.

Building Interests and Selecting Books for Children

Jean Karl

NOT ALL PARENTS are interested in whether their children learn to read. There are parents whose own educational backgrounds are such that the value of reading is not apparent to them. There are others whose own interests are so overpowering that there is no place in their thoughts for the development of their children. Yet, for most parents, it is important that a child learn the skill of reading. Far fewer are really concerned about the material read by the child once the skill has been acquired—a fact which is a sad thing. Reading is a key, a door, a passage; it can lead to good things, or it can lead nowhere.

Reading is a key to education, of course, but it can be more than that —it can also be a key to self-discovery, self-awareness, self-development, and the achievement of individuality in a world where mass production and a grey quality of sameness are an ever-present threat; that may be reading's highest value. It occurs when an interested reader finds material that involves him and becomes a part of his fund of experience.

Many parents are eager that their children finish their social studies reading assignment or complete the reading skill exercises. Few parents encourage the kind of leisure time reading that makes the more important results of reading possible. And even those who want to do so are not sure how to go about it.

The adult who wishes to encourage a child to read should know something about books and more than a little about the child's interests. A child can be read to long before he can talk, even before he can walk.

The adult should be prepared and ready to do this. Nursery rhymes and other short rhythmic pieces can be recited by the mother on impromptu occasions; the child will enjoy the swing of the words even if he does not understand them, and a sense of the rhythm of language will become a part of his first language experience.

I remember reading an article by a music critic. After the birth of their first child, he and his wife were determined that the child should enjoy music. So fine music, symphonies, concertos, string quartets, and the like were played on the phonograph every time the child was fed. I do not know how well this worked, but I did know another child who was introduced to music at a very early age. Before this child was two, he knew what he liked and could pull down a favorite record by knowing what the record cover looked like. And his tastes were sophisticated.

Children respond to what they hear and what they are exposed to. The parent who wants a book-loving child will introduce him to good books at an early age. The books he begins with will be nursery rhyme books and other books of short, simple, but good poems—not silly jingly stuff that will not do more than glance off the surface of an eager, searching mind. There will also be cloth books that small, uncoordinated hands cannot tear easily. And there will be some picture books of the usual paper, designed for use by both adult and child.

Gradually, as the child begins to master speech, there will be books with very simple stories, mirroring the child's own activities at home or at play—books like *Play With Me* by Marie Hall Etts and books that capture some of the child's emotions and questionings about the world around him, such as the best of the concept books so popular eight or ten years ago.

All of these early, simple books should be chosen with care. This is not a time to stint. It is not a time to think anything will do. If a child's basic outlook on life and the pattern of his development are set by the time he is five or six, then the books he sees and has read to him in the preceding years are important indeed. Though the content may be simple, there must be truth, honesty, and a clear sense of style in these books.

The pictures must also be tasteful. There is a place for "calendar" art, but it is not in picture books for the young. There the art—be it representational, stylized, or avantguarde in technique—should have interest in color, design, and texture as well as something to say to the immediate perception of the child who looks at it. In other words, the book should be worth looking at more than once, and continued looking should provide added pleasure and an appetite for more than surface appeal.

As the young child becomes a picture book looker and listener, his personal taste will develop in books and in other things. He will become an individual who likes some things and dislikes others. The perceptive adult will sense what is happening and will encourage the broadest possible development, giving the child opportunities to experience many things. But at the same time, the adult will recognize the child's growing individuality and see that the special books he enjoys most and the kinds of books he likes best are available, either at home or from the public library.

A child who has had this kind of experience with books at home or in a nursery school probably has a better chance of learning to read readily once he goes to school. He knows what books are. He wants to tackle them for himself. And he has a sense of "how the words come off the page" even though he cannot read them.

Once he has learned to read, the question comes, "What then shall he read?" For the beginning reader there are now many easy-to-read, I-can-read, beginner books. Few are of the literary quality of Elsa Minarick's *Little Bear,* but at this stage literary quality may not be quite as important as sheer readability. For a brief time, after a child has mastered some reading skill but has not yet developed a broad range of understanding, he needs to be encouraged to read whatever matches his reading skill. The wise parent lets the school oversee the further development of the child's reading skill and provides him with materials that give him practice and *confidence.* The parent should look for books the child can read quite easily. To the parent they may seem silly or immature, but the sheer delight in the exercise of a new power will make them fascinating to the child. The time for such books is relatively short; after a while the normal child will be ready for something more. The child should select books for himself as much as possible, just as he did with his picture books. The book a child reads at home should be as far from his school readers as possible. Though the child may find delight in being able to read almost anything, the book that holds humor, insight, beauty, adventure, or useful information will make the venture seem worthwhile.

When the child's ability and growing interest make him ready for richer experiences, the wise parent will exercise a little guidance so that the reading time will not be wasted. Generally children who read a great deal soon outgrow books and series of books that come in repetitive patterns and offer little depth and literary skill. Yet children can get caught in a rut of reading repetitive stories, such as mysteries, or reading in too limited patterns. Arguments, suggestions, or demands for better books seldom work; but good books left around, casual mention of books the adult has heard about, and the talk of friends at a library, in the classroom, or at play may stir up new interest. Adults who want to know about children's books can try the reviews in *The Horn Book,* get advice from a local children's librarian, or consult a list such as *Best Books for Children.*

Adults concerned with children who can read but do not want to read have still another problem. How does one interest such a child in reading? The answer lies in the child himself. What are his interests? Is it football in the fall, basketball in winter, and baseball in spring and summer? Do these take him out of the house and away from books at every possible opportunity? Then what about a book on how to improve his game or a book on a favorite hero? One good sport book may lead to another. Eventually books may take on some value after all. The same may be said of the horse-crazed girl, the mechanically minded boy, and the child who enjoys being in a crowd and finds the isolation of reading stifling. All children who do not read, do something. Whatever their interest, it can be matched by a book. Such children may never become continual readers, but they need not miss books altogether.

A few children do not learn to read at all. They may have some physical disorder that prevents it; they may have mental blocks that impede them; they may simply see no reason at all to exert the effort. Whatever the cause, the concerned adult must show sympathy and willingness to help and provide a substitution for reading when requested. But there should never be condemnation or reproof. The books made available to such a child should be books that will not seem babyish but that will, through pictures, give him ideas. Records and audio tapes may help. Whatever is done should be encouraging and not discouraging. Suitable adult magazines with many pictures—sports magazines and the like— may be a substitute in some areas of experience. It is what this child may be able to read, or what he wants to read, and not what he cannot read that should be important. Again the question of what books he should be introduced to can be answered only by a deep knowledge of what the child is. The answer cannot come from what the adult wishes a child would be or thinks he ought to be.

For all children, from vociferous readers to nonreaders, the books that will appeal can be determined only by the child himself and what he is as a person. Children are not small blobs of playdough to be molded to an adult's desire. Instead, children are small units of potential who must be permitted to determine their own courses to some extent. Adults can draw out a child's interests, enlarge upon them, and encourage new interests, but adults cannot make an interest. The job of the adult is to know the child, and then to make the books available or make a source for the books available, and to help the child know how to select books. The book most likely to be read is the book the child himself has selected, provided he has selected wisely. He needs to know that the cover, the pictures, and the first line of text are not always an adequate guide and that sometimes even books that interest him can be too simple to hold his continued interest or too difficult to do more than frustrate him.

The adult who is going to buy a book for a child may want to buy a book that the child has already had from the library and longs to own for ready rereading. But if this purchase is not possible, then the adult who is selecting a book for a child should look for a true book of excellence in some area he knows the child will enjoy.

How does one know a book of excellence? One asks a librarian or other qualified person. One reads reviews, good reviews, in such media as *Horn Book, Bulletin of the Materials Center at the University of Chicago,* and *Young Reader's Review;* in lists such as those done by NCTB and *Best Books for Children;* or other professional sources. Or one examines what is available. There is no yardstick for quickly and consistently identifying a book of excellence, but the following guidelines may help in making a choice.

If the adult is selecting fiction and must do it with no help other than his own eyes and a group of books, the first thing to do is to identify those books that may be of interest to the child. Obviously a teenage romance is not going to fascinate an eight-year-old boy, for example. With those that seem likely candidates, the adult should read a bit here and there through each book and ask himself: Do the people sound like real people? Do the situations sound genuine or are they sentimentalized, slick and superficial, or perhaps overdramatized? Are the ideas in the book modern enough for a child or young person of today? Is the setting real or is the author merely hanging a backdrop for the action? Does the book seem as if it is going to be worth the time spent reading it? Is the writing style good? Does the action begin quickly? Is the reading level about right for the interested reader?

Many of these things can be determined quite quickly by a perceptive adult. Poor writing can be seen in one sampling. Poor characters and conversations are not hard to recognize. Depth and originality of ideas are harder to identify in a brief analysis, but the possibility of their presence can at least be determined by the subject matter.

The adult may also look at the frame of the book, the illustrations, and the design. Do they suit the child and the book? And are they tasteful? Will they subtly build in a reader an appreciation of good things? These are only a few of the criteria for judging a good book, of course. Put into action, however, they would assure fewer *un*read gift books.

The adult selecting nonfiction should first find those books that may be within a child's interest and reading range. Then he should examine the scope of each book. Does it cover so much area in such a small space that it cannot possibly say anything of lasting value, or does it examine in a long book such a minute area that the child will be bored? If either is true, the book is not right. The area covered in the book should be well chosen for the length of the book and the reading level. And within that area chosen, the material should be well organized. It should begin at the beginning and go on to a logical stopping place. A table of contents will often reveal this. The writing should be clear and precise. It should make the ideas the author is presenting plain. And the illustrations should be clear and relevant. They should fit the text, enlarging and developing the ideas the author has presented. There should be a glossary, if it is needed; an index; suggestions for further reading. Most adults are not equipped to judge the accuracy of books of nonfiction, except those on the most elementary level; but the presence of a glossary, an index, a list for further reading, or other necessary appendages can indicate the seriousness of the author in preparing his work. Finally, the adult should ask if the book is attractive, for even in nonfiction attractiveness is important.

All of these criteria, if followed, will insure the thoughtful selection of a book for a child. And the adult, by catering to the good and to what is unique in the child, will be helping the child through his reading to become a unique person. By speaking casually about books in his general conversations, by his own reading, and by having books around as a normal part of the environment, the adult can help further by making reading seem attractive and desirable. He can give subtle and responsive guidance, always gently enlarging the child's interest but never forcing.

Books can be any child's richest experience. The slum child who sees the world beyond his limited environment may be inspired to seek a way out for himself and others. On the other hand, when he sees his own world mirrored in a book, he will learn that he is not alone in his problems. The more privileged child who is led into other environments and other cultures by books may not show the prejudices of his parents. Children with all the earthly comforts they need can find that others do not share their good fortune. They can also discern some things that others may have and they do not, so they will not be too smug. Young scientists may plumb the depth of their understanding; young musicians may learn of other musicians; and young carpenters may see what they can build. And maybe all can be led eventually to see something beyond themselves and their primary interests. This is one of the great values of reading, along with the pleasuré of reading—a pleasure, once discovered, that can last the rest of an individual's life, whatever his fortune.

A Parent's Concern—
Questions Parents Ask

Elizabeth Hendryson

As A LAYMAN at a conference of professionals, it is especially gratifying to confer with other professional laymen from the PTA to enlarge the dialogue between the parents, whom we represent, and the teachers of reading.

In this presentation I'll ask questions that I've heard parents ask. I hope you will answer them in your respective schools and give the parents there opportunities to raise other questions.

Although I speak for parents in this colloquy, I cannot pretend that I am today's average parent because my life has been marked by a series of reading serendipities which, when added together, constitute a course in how to teach reading. So I am speaking now as this kind of expert— what behavioral scientists call experiential and I call life-trained.

My own experience is rooted in reading because my generation was a reading generation. As a little girl in Pittsburgh, Pennsylvania, I walked two miles to the public library almost every afternoon. My orientation was to books as recreation and to the library as the center of this recreation.

Then I have the kind of experience that comes to an overconscientious parent. When my first baby came along, an encyclopedia salesman sold me a set of *Childcraft* along with promises about what *Childcraft* would do for me as a mother making her way uncertainly through a maze of decisions and activities, each of which I knew would have a profound and ineradicable influence on my child as he grew up. I pledged $3 a month out of my meager household budget and addressed myself to reading every single word. Also, I began a small collection of books on the care and feeding of babies.

By the time my son was nine months old, I was stunned to learn that, beginning at the age of six months, I should have been reading nursery rhymes aloud to him regularly. I feared for the irrevocable damage that must already have been done to him during the three months that had gone by. When I started reading, I felt silly reading nursery rhymes to him; but the magic worked. He loved them.

The encyclopedia further stated that one should read good stories to his child every night. Dutifully I read to that little boy every night until he could read to himself; and if I did not read, my husband did. When we went out, the babysitter read.

In that edition of *Childcraft* I read that a parent must *never* teach a child to read a single word, the parent's function being to provide readiness experiences—such as taking the child places and then talking to him about the things he saw—so he could become skillful in the use of language. I cheated because Peter would often ask me, "What is that word?" I don't know how he knew that there were words there, but somehow he got the idea. I would tell him, and then I'd feel guilty for days because I was sure that he probably had learned the wrong way to identify this word. The fact that he could identify words on signboards puzzled me terribly because according to a theory I had read, he was not supposed to be able to. You can see that a young, inexperienced, well-meaning mother will swallow anything. I believed that everybody is ready to read at the same time and the same process is right for teaching every child.

When my two children went to school, I learned that there was a way of teaching reading—the only way as far as I was concerned—which was a word identification method. Both children learned to read immediately; therefore, as far as I knew, this was *the* method, and I never questioned the divine wisdom of the singular method system.

In 1955 I became chairman of the National PTA Committee on Reading and Library Service. I began my service at the beginning of the reading controversy that was stirred up by Rudolf Flesch with his publication of *Why Johnny Can't Read*. As far as most parents were concerned, Flesch was the first person to draw attention to the fact that a difference of opinion existed among teachers about how reading should be taught. His theorizing that phonics was the only method for all teaching of reading was so emphatic that a sort of sanctification of phonics ensued.

The mass media have been most influential in propagating the blindest faith among parents in the magic of phonics as a method of teaching children to read. During the epidemic of phonics fever of the mid 50s, numerous courses for parents who wanted to teach their children phonics were published in the popular press, along with dozens of articles by Flesch and his followers. Public reaction to Flesch's book was unbelievable, and immediately following publication the teaching of reading became the surprising topic of social conversation.

Very shortly most of the PTA meetings I went to or read about had programs devoted to "How is reading taught in our school?" I discovered that in spite of Flesch's saying phonics was not taught anywhere, phonics *was* being taught, along with word identification methods. And most children seemed to be learning to read quite well.

The impact of Flesch's book illustrates the interest that many parents take in their children's education. The outbreak at the Ocean Hill-Brownsville School District is a dramatic illustration of this interest. As teachers know, most parents are continually measuring a teacher's competency, generally by observation of their children's progress in school. Unfortunately, parents do not have a very good measure to apply besides the grades their children receive, and parents do not always understand grading systems. The one measure that we parents think we can understand is a child's reading ability. If we know a child can read, we think we can tell that he is succeeding. Unfortunately, our own interpretation of this measure is based on fuzzy memories of how we, ourselves, learned to read.

Parents seldom blame themselves when their children do not learn to read or do not succeed in school. Yet we now know that parents can have an influence on whether children learn to read. It is the teacher's challenge to inform parents of their responsibilities.

While teachers are wondering how to educate parents, the mass media —that "pop" adult educator of our time—keep the public informed about their versions of the new developments in the field of reading instruction.

For instance, recently the press and partisans of the phonics method publicized the results of an apparently sound survey by Jeanne Chall. However, most of the reviews I have read question the validity of some of Chall's conclusions. Many of my friends, having received their information from the mass media, are crowing that she "proved conclusively" that "phonics" is the *only* way to teach reading successfully. Other reading innovations publicized by the mass media range from the Initial Teaching Alphabet and Individually Prescribed Instruction to preschool reading and speed reading courses.

All of this information is terribly confusing for parents. We need authorities in reading to answer some of the questions that keep bothering us. For example, in view of the pervasive influence of television everywhere and the widespread use of audiovisual material, parents ask if reading is really necessary anymore. I am making the assumption that the answer is "yes;" reading and the use of language still form the foundation of the education process. My faith in this firm fact has been shaken in recent years, as perhaps yours has been, by the various pronouncements of Marshall McLuhan, Margaret Mead, and their disciples. No matter what they say, everything leads to the conclusion that reading now and for some time to come is going to be the foundation of the learning process. I believe this statement implicitly in spite of the fact that the education meetings I have attended for the past four or five years have seemed to reflect the machine age in the classroom as well as everywhere else in our society. In fact, there has been so much emphasis on programed learning, TV teaching, and other mechanical means of presenting materials to young people that someone at the 1960 White House Conference on Children and Youth predicted in the year 2,000 the Ford Foundation would undertake a study to determine the feasibility of having a live teacher in every classroom!

Francis Chase developed a thesis that it is the primary challenge of education in the 60s to see that every child between two and six years is read to from a book by "someone he loves" as the absolute prerequisite to learning in school.

By "someone he loves," Chase refers to the adults with whom the child identifies positively—his parents, his older brothers and sisters, his grandparents, or anyone whom he wishes to emulate. If the admired or loved adult reads books for his own pleasure and information, he communicates to the child the belief that in books there is something for him, too. Especially if the adult reads to the child from a book and shares some delightful experience with him, then the child himself is motivated when he goes to school. When the ultimatum "Now you will learn to read" is handed down, he knows that within the covers of books there is something delicious for him.

Chase departed from this thesis to say that some educators have to guarantee that these opportunities are provided for children because obviously a vast majority of children do not have an adult whom they love and who reads to them before going to school. Chase suggested that perhaps we should organize senior citizens, who are appealing to children and are usually eager to be of use in the community, to go into all kinds of neighborhoods and read from a book to children.

He kept emphasizing "from a book," which is an answer to another question asked by many parents: "Don't children have these acculturating experiences through their viewing of TV?" In explanation, Chase pointed out that the dynamic interaction between adults and children in motivating a child to learn to read is not there when one is getting stimuli from a machine. Television experiences are not book-related; they do not serve the purpose of motivating to read.

Parents who are concerned about preparing children for school, as PTA parents are, ask floods of questions, among them:

- If these vital, early childhood experiences are so good for poor children, aren't they necessary for all children? And if so, how can we provide these experiences for all children in all neighborhoods?
- How much should we teach our children before they go to school? Where can we learn how to teach them? *Should* we teach them?
- If I can't teach my child to learn to read before he goes to school, will he ever catch up with the children who did learn early?
- What are "good" books for my child? Where can I get a list of them? Where can I buy or borrow them?
- Which reading method is best? Which one is being used to teach my child? Who takes the first step in arranging PTA programs on reading, the parent or the teacher?
- Why doesn't our school have a library? (This is one of the questions most frequently asked in individual PTAs.)

It seems that providing "good" books for children in an easily accessible place has become part of the modern social dilemma. But I found one of the answers in a clipping from a recent *Chicago Tribune*. In a ghetto school there is a program called "Read, Baby, Read." And what is it? As you might suspect, it has nothing to do with learning to read in a reader, but it provides a wide range of paperbacks on various subjects and various kinds of literature for children. There is a club with set goals appropriate to reading levels of the students and with points given for the number of books read. It was found that the children were so fascinated with the reading made available to them that almost every grade had more than double the ultimate number of points before the program was half over.

- Are such programs desirable or necessary?
- How can I tell if my child is learning? If not, why not? What is dyslexia? Is someone testing to see if my child has it?
- Will it improve my child's reading if he takes a speed reading course? (The sensational newspaper writing that promises miracles in increasing reading speed has put another burden on parents who want their children to read well.) How can I evaluate new developments in reading instruction?
- What should I be doing at home to help my child learn to read? Is he getting enough phonics?

In conclusion, I repeat that it is clear that parents are partners in this important project. I know teachers will agree with me that they cannot successfully teach without parents as partners. So I urge teachers to help the PTA and other parent groups to carry out the mission of interpreting reading methods. The PTA does it through programs and institutes at its own conventions; *The PTA Magazine* has included articles which interpret all of these developments in the teaching of reading over the years, and one of the four priority action programs of the next national PTA administration will be devoted to reading improvement services everywhere. Because the PTA is an adult education organization, we try to provide opportunities for parents to learn what their responsibilities are. However, the PTA cannot be effective unless teachers are active in the education process of their built-in partners, the parents.

I urge you teachers not to let parents flounder around, trying to find out what is going on in the area of reading. Court us a little; disseminate to us some of your professional knowledge; interpret for us what you are doing and what you expect of us as parents.

I also warn you of the obvious: If you do not answer the questions parents ask, if you do not enable parents to make a positive contribution, they may contribute negatively. Let us all meet our challenge on the firmest foundation we can provide—that of working together.

Teaching Parents to Help at Home

Alma Harrington

SCHOOLS CANNOT and would not exist without parents. Parents supply the school with primary material—their children—around which the formal educational and organizational program for that school is constructed. The main purpose of a school is to provide formal training or learning experiences that will educate an individual. To put it another way, in school each child is instructed and exposed to specific programs and activities designed to increase his background of knowledge and learning. Generally, each one of our states has set a specific chronological age at which each child must begin attending a school to become involved with a program of formal learning instruction. This statement does not mean that prior to the child's attaining school age he has not begun to learn; for learning is the acquisition of knowledge or understanding, and it cannot be limited to beginning at one specific age. In fact, in a broad sense, learning may be said to begin the moment a child is born. When a child reaches school age, he will leave his home or residential situation for six to eight hours, five days each week, to become involved in activities in school. However, even after a child reaches school age, he is still involved with his home or residential situation for the other 16 to 18 hours in each day, plus the weekends.

People—parents and children—are members of a given society or social class. Each member of a society is involved in some type of home or residential situation. The customs and standards that a particular society will have and use are determined by its members. Generally, the children within a given society or community are brought together for formal learning experiences within a school. In other words, every child in a community is involved in both a school and a residential situation.

Traditionally, parents send their children to school to receive formal educational training. In school the child is exposed to material which is designed to build up and expand his background of knowledge. Periodically, the parents are contacted by the school system. This contact may involve the obtaining of specific information about the child, or it may concern the communication to the parents of specific information pertaining to the child. This direct contact with each parent is usually carried out by means of phone calls, report cards, notes, or conferences. At times the school personnel hold an informational meeting related to their operational program. This meeting may be for the total community or society in which the school is located, or it may be held for a small group of individuals for whom the information is relevant. PTA groups are formed to involve the total community in what is happening or being carried out in school.

Periodically, parents ask teachers questions, such as, "Johnny seems to be behind in reading. What can I do at home to help him?" Sometimes the parents are given specific, helpful suggestions as an answer to their question. There are other times, however, when the parents receive such answers as "Oh, don't worry about it. He will grow out of it!" or "We know what Johnny needs. Let us take care of it." Sometimes parents ask a particular school system or teacher to explain why one method of instruction rather than another is used. Or, parents ask school personnel to give a specific explanation of how the school system teaches reading or another designated subject. Sometimes parents receive satisfactory answers to these questions. There are times, however, when parents receive no answer from the school personnel or answers similar to the following: "We know what instructional method or program is best for your child; don't question our judgment." "We'll explain this method to you, but you probably won't understand it because you don't possess our background of knowledge for this area," or "It's one of the latest techniques; other places have had a lot of success with this approach." The frequency with which parents and individuals are beginning to question specific practices within school systems is increasing. These questions arise particularly at three points in a year: 1) when the school budget comes up for voter approval; 2) when the school tax notices are sent out; and 3) when a parent's child encounters difficulty in or with a learning situation.

School personnel are becoming more alert to, and aware of, parents and their questions. More and more these professionals are realizing the tremendous impact that a child's home situation and his parents can have upon that individual's ultimate learning development. Repeatedly, school personnel see instances when the amount of learning attained by a child is either minimized, negated, or obliterated because of harmful factors within the home, the school, or both. For instance, suppose that in school a child is taught to figure out an unknown word by thinking of the sounds of the first and last letters and, with these clues, to determine what word fits the context. Perhaps this child might read to his parents and, when doing so, utilize this same method to identify words he does not know. However, suppose that his mother tells the child that this approach is very slow and that a better way is to either skip the word or to memorize the whole word. This new direction creates a dilemma for the child. Not only is he confronted with two different approaches to learning but also he must make a decision about which authority to listen to and follow.

One of the basic goals forming part of the foundation underlying public school education in this country is the improvement, upgrading, and influencing of our society and the individuals within it. School personnel are realizing that this goal cannot be achieved unless both home and school settings are directly involved with each other in learning experiences. The need for more operational programs utilizing this belief exists today.

Many specific ideas have come to mind for improving communications and relations between the home and school. This past year it was my privilege to be able to implement and try out one of these ideas—namely, the construction of a course for parents, "Helping Children with Reading in the Home." This concept is not a one-night meeting for parents upon this subject. Rather, it is a specific, informational, background course in reading which was implemented as an adult education course for the Hamburg, New York, Central School. The course contains information pertaining to skills involved in the act of reading and suggests specific activities appropriate for the home that would be useful for strengthening reading development.

When it was originally formulated, the course consisted of ten sessions with a designated topic pertaining to reading for each session. However, the preliminary response to the initial publicity for the course seemed to indicate that the parents were hesitant about signing up for a ten-week course. So, the promotional approach for engaging parents in course work pertaining to the field of reading was changed. An announcement was made that all adults interested in attending a few class sessions related to reading instruction were to meet on a specified night. At this meeting, a discussion was conducted which centered around the topics that the parents would like to have included in future class sessions.

From their comments and suggestions, five specific topics were formed as the basis for future instructional class sessions. These topics were as follows: "Reading—What It Involves and Various Approaches to It," "Preschool Preparatory Experiences," "Reading Instruction in Grades One to Three," "Reading Instruction in Grades Four to Six," and "Library Books and Their Use by Children at Home." The same five topics are used as the basic outline at the present time.

Specific material has been written for each topic included in the course outline.* The material for each topic was formulated with four specific aims in mind: 1) to provide the parents with specific background information for that topic; 2) to provide helpful tips for working with skills pertaining to that topic; 3) to suggest activities related to that topic which can easily be used and implemented within the home situation; and 4) to refer, only casually, to published materials which the parents could buy in relation to that topic.

The first topic for the course, "Reading—What It Involves and Various Approaches to It," provides the participants with information on what is included in the process of learning to read. One of the first activities in which the parents become involved is to read a cartoon. Then they answer specific questions in relation to what they did when they read the cartoon. Their answers are discussed with them. This discussion leads to teaching and illustrating various individual actions and responses that are involved with reading. A special diagram illustrating these areas is drawn for the participants so they can more easily understand this information. A brief description of the various approaches and methods used for teaching reading is given. Sample materials from various companies are used as illustrative material during the discussion. Definitions are included for some of the terms that the parents may have heard or that they may hear used in future class sessions.

The topic "Preschool Preparatory Experiences" centers around the child and his experiences from birth to the point at which he begins his formal reading experience within the school situation. The characteristic criteria, or list of characteristics which many schools use for determining whether a child is ready to begin to formally learn to read, are used as the basis for class discussions and instruction. The instructional material of this topic is divided into six subtopics: physical development, social development, language development, emotional development, mental development, and experiential background. Each subtopic contains background information, aims toward which the parent should work in the child's development, and suggested activities for implementation in the home situation.

One example of the type of activity suggested for this area is the following:

* *How to Help Your Child with Reading at Home,* by Alma Harrington. (Available from author for $3.50.)

Sandwich Learning. Let the child make his favorite sandwich for lunch; then cut off the crusts so that the bread is square and use it to help the child distinguish various shapes and sizes. First, name the shape of the sandwich and show the child that it is a square. Then cut the square on a diagonal into two triangles. Discuss the shapes.

"Reading in Grades One to Three" includes a discussion of the reading skills usually taught in the first three grades in most public schools in this country. The skill areas included are word attack and word recognition, phonics, comprehension, and interpretation. Each subtopic includes a discussion of background information and helpful tips pertinent to that skill, guidelines for practicing and building up that skill, and suggested activities for the home in relation to that skill.

"Reading in Grades Four to Six" includes information pertaining to the reading skills usually emphasized in the fourth through sixth grades in most public schools. The subtopics used are interpretation of material that is read, using various types of reference books, and work-study skills which relate to reading. Each subtopic includes a discussion of relevant background information, guidelines for practicing and building up that topic, and suggested related activities for the home.

"Library Books and Their Use by Children at Home" includes a list of some books which a child might enjoy reading. These books are compiled in developmental reading levels comparable to the way a child's reading ability might develop. The material for this topic also includes tips for guiding the child in selecting books. Information is presented in relation to various types of books available for the child to read. Guidelines for listening to a child read aloud in the home situation are discussed. Creative ideas for encouraging a child's interest in reading are included.

Informational material pertaining to each topic is duplicated and given to the participants during the course sessions. Further suggestions and explanations are given as each topic is discussed. During the first session the participants receive a bibliography of books and pamphlets that relate to the subject of the parent and reading. This list of materials is not required reading but a suggested way for parents to broaden their backgrounds.

Sometimes parents are asked to bring specific materials from their homes to use in simulated learning activities. Such materials might include cookie cutters, catalogs, magazines, sandpaper, or pieces of cardboard. Sometimes part of the class session is spent in constructing instructional devices for use in the homes. Commercial materials are suggested, but this course does not emphasize the use of this type of material.

The number of actual class sessions involved in covering and discussing the information contained in the five topical areas is determined by the participants. The first time the course was taught it was held for six sessions; the second time, for ten. Each session usually runs for two hours. The first one and one-half hours are devoted to the instruction and discussion of the material pertaining to that session's topic. The last half hour is questioning time.

The participants in this course are not taught to assume the role or responsibility of the teacher or provide a formal instructional situation. Rather, the parents are advised to reinforce or work with the teacher(s) with whom their child is involved.

The backgrounds of the participating individuals were varied. Most of the parents had little formal educational training beyond high school. Some parents had only preschool children. Sometimes, only one parent attended. One participant was a trained junior high school reading teacher; another, a volunteer helper in reading. Many members had at least one child experiencing a difficulty with reading at that time.

The results of an evaluative questionnaire completed at the end of the class sessions show that all the participants found the course material of benefit. Specific aspects which they stated as the most beneficial included: the detailed background given for prereading experiences, the opinions or theories on dealing with children that were given by the instructor, knowing what the child might be taught in school on reading, the information on the methods of teaching reading that are used in schools, the tips and activities given for improving a child's reading, the suggested books a child might read for himself, the printed notes on each section for easy referral, the written and oral instruction involved in the class sessions, the tips for correcting reading difficulties, and the guidelines for building a child's background in phonics.

The opinions of the parents vary as to which topic or subtopic in the course was the most valuable. Their specific selections included prereading experiences, the sequence of reading skill development, specific suggestions that could be used at home for how parents can help, the entire course, the experience of identifying with a "beginning reading" situation, the theories of learning given during the instructional sessions, and the specific techniques for figuring out words.

Further comments of parents:

- Finding out that there are ways of helping my child at home is very gratifying. I constantly refer to the materials received. If one approach does not work with my child, I look through the notes for another approach. I can now keep his interest for a short time without boring him. I am very pleased about the many helps I received from this course.
- I now feel more confident in helping my children at home with their

reading. My two preschoolers will start school with a better prereading development than did my two older children.

- My contact with a concerned trained person who deals with children for their benefit has been a most rewarding experience. Mothers tend to become so concerned with their own children and their problems that they fail to see the child in relation to others.
- This class seemed to benefit and flourish in the informal atmosphere that was provided. It is especially nice to find a teacher who feels that parents are educable.

CONCLUSION

Teaching a parent is no different from teaching any other individual. The participants in this course have usually come seeking simple, workable, specific information and activities to use and understand. The parents seemed willing to take the time to help their children with reading after obtaining an understanding of 1) what to do and 2) how this activity could be worked into the regular functioning of their home.

Some individuals reading this article may be apprehensive about allowing parents to participate in a course containing background information pertaining to teaching a specific subject because of the duplication of activities which might occur within the home and school. However, in this course emphasis is placed upon the fact that each reading skill is best introduced in the school by a professional teacher. But, once the skill has been introduced, it should be practiced and built up in both the school and the home. Real learning does not occur with only one encounter. Rather, learning is reinforced through repetition. For instance, think how many times you hear and say a commercial advertisement before you have actually learned it so that you can repeat it from memory. All the activities suggested to the parents in relation to this course usually involve materials and items generally found in the home. Although the same skill may be included in the instruction that the child receives in school, generally the materials used in practice will be different.

Closer involvement and communication between the home and school could become a most enjoyable, exciting, and challenging area because most parents are quite interested in learning how to teach their children.

The following hints on how parents can help are from the author's previously mentioned booklet:

1. Make sure your child has sufficient rest each night. Get him to bed early.
2. See that your child is not rushed off to school in the morning in an unhappy mood.

3. Do not compare your child's progress with that of other children—brothers, sisters, or the child next door. Each child is an individual with his own pattern and rate of learning.

4. Be genuinely interested in the work which your child brings home. Your interest will make him want to do his best work.

5. Do read to your child, even though he may be able to enjoy books by himself.

6. Take your child to the library regularly and let him browse among the books in the children's section.

7. Be a good listener. Set aside a few minutes each evening for the child who wants to tell you what he has done in school.

8. Make your child feel that you enjoy listening to him read. No matter how simple the story, show an interest in what happens.

9. Praise your child when he puts forth a real effort to do his best.

10. Help your child to read with expression—just the way he would talk. Make sure he chooses stories with words that are easy for him to read aloud.

11. Make it a privilege for a younger brother or sister to hear your child read a story.

12. Share the reading aloud of a story with your child. For instance, you read one page and he reads the next page. It will help him to improve his expression and gain more confidence.

13. Ask questions about the story to make sure that your child is getting the meaning. If he cannot remember what he has read or answer questions about material read, he is not really reading. He is only word calling.

14. Help your child to add words to his speaking vocabulary. The larger number of words he can use naturally, in everyday conversation, the more meanings for words he will know when he sees a specific word in a book.

15. Play word games—such as rhyming words, words beginning with the same sound, or "I'm thinking of a word . . ."—with your child.

Early Start in Reading—
Help or Hindrance?*

Joseph E. Brzeinski
and
Helen N. Driscoll

THE DENVER PUBLIC SCHOOLS, with the aid of a grant from the Carnegie Corporation of New York, conducted a research study to determine how effectively parents can prepare their preschool children for reading. The rationale for this study is found in conditions of the world today.

The world as it is today requires the learning and application of an unprecedented amount of complex information. Therefore, improvement in the efficiency of the total educational process is urgently needed. One way to increase the efficiency of education is to give children an earlier and better start in reading. Research evidence suggests that some children are capable of beginning reading activities much earlier than they customarily do start.

Parents in today's world tend to carry on many informal activities which contribute to their children's early and effective reading. The Denver Public Schools use a systematic, organized procedure for conducting these activities which, at the kindergarten level, has shown promise.

A research project was therefore designed to find out whether parents, with suitable professional assistance and direction, could employ the procedure as adapted for home use and whether their children might start reading even earlier than kindergarten.

* The research reported herein was supported by the Cooperative Research Program of the Office of Education, U. S. Department of Health, Education, and Welfare and by the Carnegie Corporation of New York.

Hypotheses

Specifically, three hypotheses were tested:

1. Prior to their entrance into school children can learn skills which are basic to beginning reading.
2. Parents can and will use the beginning reading techniques which are presented by way of educational television, the use of 16mm films, and the use of parent-direction manuals to teach basic reading skills to their children at home.
3. There will be no significant difference in learning to read between children whose parents are taught beginning reading techniques by watching television and those whose parents are taught these techniques by experienced teachers using 16mm films of the television programs in small parent-education groups.

Supporting Evidence

This study has been based upon the recognition that no one mental age is a guarantee of success in beginning reading. Equally important are the methods and materials used (*16*). Experimental studies have shown that children have been taught to read as early as ages three, four, five, and six. In Scotland, children are regularly introduced to reading at age five (*6*).

Research indicates that the best readers and the first to learn to read are usually those children who know the most letter forms and sounds (*31*).

Studies have shown that there is a significant, positive relationship between the opportunities to learn to read which children have before they enter first grade and their later success in beginning reading. Being read to, looking at books and other printed material, and similar activities make a significant contribution to the preparation of a child for beginning reading instruction. However, children's interest in letters, words, and numbers is also very important in this preparation (*1*).

A study of children who learned to read at home showed that these children were reading at grade levels ranging from 1.5 to 4.6 with a mean of 2.3 when they entered first grade. In all of the cases of children who knew how to read prior to entering school, someone was found in the family who had been willing and able to teach interested youngsters to read (*12*).

A preliminary report of reading research, jointly financed by the Denver Public School and the Cooperative Research Branch of the United

States Office of Education, shows that kindergarten-age children can be taught the skills basic to learning to read (7).

Before they enter first grade, most children have had some variety of home reading instruction which has grown out of the things the child notices in his everyday living. When the child is read to, there is a tendency for the parents to make explanations and to point out words. Some parents ask the children to read to them. When children show an interest in words or letters or numbers around them, parents tend to have them repeat the experience and seize on any opportunity for teaching. When the child begins to notice labels on cans for example, the parent may point out whole words or initial letters or may spell out words letter by letter. He is likely to check on the child's learning the next time opportunity arises by having the child find the can with that label. When the parent sees a sign or word which the child has noticed before, he is likely to call the child's attention to it (1).

Prevailing Concerns

Critics state that providing beginning reading experiences prior to first grade may ultimately cause certain reading disabilities, such as poor reading habits, dislike or even withdrawal from reading, and possible visual defects.

Claims that the eyes of children are not mature enough for them to begin to read safely at the usual ages of entrance into school are inconclusive. In a recent study by Eames, it was found that five-year-old children have more accommodative power visually than at any age thereafter. Among the children Eames studied, the poorest visual acuity found was quite sufficient for reading the usual textbooks (14).

Evidence has been presented which indicates that the normal child of a mental age of five to six years can perceive simple forms without difficulty (30). Reading difficulties are usually brought about by several contributing factors rather than just one isolated cause. Studies of the causes of reading difficulties provide no evidence of clear-cut factors which are found only in poor readers but never in good readers (22).

Other critics of earlier introduction to the skills which are basic to beginning reading point out that the child who exhibits an early interest in reading is frequently encouraged by the parent to pursue this interest at the expense of some other aspect of his development. However, it does not follow that such a situation can be avoided only by prohibiting early reading experience.

Because of this possibility of misplaced emphasis, parents participating in the study were repeatedly cautioned that these instructional activities should be guided by the readiness and receptiveness of their individual children. Instruction should be given only when the child displays an interest in the activities and when they fit into the normal activities of the family and are an outgrowth of the natural experiences of the child.

An effective program of beginning reading instruction should be, first of all, a good program for young children. It will accept and respect children for all kinds of learning. In such a program there is little danger of losing perspective on the place of reading in the lives of children (*1*).

Treatment Groups

In order that a basis might be established for testing the hypotheses and evaluating this approach to the teaching of the skills which are basic to beginning reading, three treatment groups of children and parents participating in the study were used:

- Group X. Parents received no instruction in teaching the basic reading skills. However, the children took the same tests as those in the other groups in order to distinguish between reading development as a result of teaching and reading development which might occur as the result of maturation.
- Group Y. Parents were provided instruction for teaching the basic reading skills through the use of a guidebook and educational television lessons.
- Group Z. The parents were provided instruction for teaching the basic reading skills by means of the guidebook and 16mm films of the television lessons.

The Reading Method

The reading method used in this study was developed by Paul McKee and M. Lucile Harrison of Colorado State College, Greeley, Colorado. The activities were designed for use by parents. The method makes use of oral words the child already knows so that he can learn the skills which are basic to beginning reading. It is made up of the following steps or skills:

1. Giving children practice in using something said (spoken or read) to call to mind any word that could come next to make sense.
2. Giving children practice in listening for consonant sounds at the beginning of words spoken (by parent or child) to teach what is meant by the beginning of a spoken word.

3. Giving children practice in distinguishing the letter forms from one another and learning the letter names.
4. Teaching children the letter-sound associations for certain consonants.
5. Giving children practice in using together something said (spoken or read aloud) and the beginning consonant letter or letters (shown) to call to mind a word that is omitted.
6. Giving children practice in using together something said (spoken or read aloud) and the beginning consonant letter or letters in a printed word (shown) to decide what that word is.

Subjects

The organization of the Denver Public Schools includes an established preschool program from which subjects for this study could be readily recruited. These classes met on alternate weeks for one half-day with parents and their prekindergarten children in attendance. The instructional program for the parents was directed by full-time professional teachers. The children met in a room separate from the parents and engaged in typical nursery school activities under supervision.

Membership in any one class was limited to children who were three or four years old in September of the current year. Depending upon the location within the city, average class size ranged from 20 to 28 children. Enrollment by parent and child was a condition of participation by either.

Since the instructional phase of the study was developed primarily for young children prior to their entrance in school, the involvement of parents and children in the organized preschool classes would provide enough volunteer participants to furnish reliable information; make available large numbers of people with whom communication procedures had already been established; and provide groups representative of all socio-economic areas of the city.

Procedure

The support of the Denver County Council of Parent Teacher Associations was enlisted to inform people of the study and to set up a suggested operational procedure on the local school level.

With the assistance of the PTA and preschool teachers, a sufficient number of parent volunteers, with their children, was obtained.

The guidebook for parents presented the basic instructional plan. It contained special materials necessary for this instruction but not normally found in the home. The suggestions and materials were organized in sixteen chapters or sections designed to enable parents to follow all six steps in the procedure.

The instructional content of the 16 television programs was similar to that of the 16 lessons in the guidebook. An experienced television teacher presented each lesson to the viewers. To demonstrate actual teaching of the skill or activity in the lesson, a television "family" consisting of a father, a mother, and two small children was used.

Kinescopes of the television lessons were shown to parents in the parent education classes conducted in conjunction with the Denver preschool program. These classes led by experienced teachers met on alternate weeks to view two of the lessons and discuss them. Purpose of this procedure was to determine if the reading activities could be presented effectively on film in communities lacking educational television facilities.

The instructional programs for parents continued for a total of sixteen weeks. These programs were essentially an adult education course and progressed at a rate suitable to the adult level. As was emphasized in the guide and in the programs, children were not expected to proceed at this rate. Parents were cautioned to work with their children at the rate established by the child's ability and interest.

Psychological Tests

To determine the relationship between academic aptitude (IQ) and the performance of the children on a test of the basic skills to be administered at the conclusion of the instruction and to compensate for the differences between groups caused by this potential during the statistical phase of the study, the children were given the Stanford-Binet Test (Form LM, 1960 Revision). The services of school staff psychologists were secured for this very important part of the research. The testing was begun in October and completed by the second week in March.

Test of Basic Skills

In order that the effects of the instruction on the children's knowledge of the skills basic to beginning reading might be determined, it was necessary to secure an evaluative instrument which would be appropriate for this purpose.

After considerable study, Tests 3 and 5 of the Test of Skills Basic to Beginning Reading, published by Houghton Mifflin, were selected as the evaluative instruments. Test 3 is a measure of the child's knowledge of letter names, both capital and small, as they are read aloud. Test 5 measures the child's ability to match letters and sounds.

Parent Survey

To determine the response of the parents to this program, the helpfulness of the instruction which had been given, and their feelings about the worth of these activities, a special questionnaire was prepared and administered during the two-week period when the children were being tested.

Of the large number of people throughout the country who had written the Denver Public Schools requesting a copy of the parent guidebook, two thousand, selected at random, were mailed a similar questionnaire to secure their appraisal of the guidebook and their feelings about the value of the instruction provided.

RESULTS AND CONCLUSIONS

Tests of Hypotheses

Hypothesis one, that parents will use the beginning reading techniques to teach their preschool children at home, was verified. Hypothesis two, that children taught by parents using the beginning reading techniques will make significantly greater progress than children in control groups in learning the skills basic to beginning reading, also was verified. The real value of home instruction is more accurately indicated when the performance of children who had more than 30 minutes of practice per week is compared to that of children who had 30 minutes or less. This highly significant result indicates the value of the prescribed home instruction and shows quite clearly that the key to success, so far as the subject matter of this project is concerned, is practice—the critical amount of practice being more than 30 minutes per week.

Hypothesis three, that there would be no significant difference between children whose parents were taught the beginning reading techniques by television and those whose parents were taught by experienced teachers using 16mm films of the programs, also was verified.

Parental Interest and Its Relation to Performance

Parents involved in the project gave it overwhelming approval. Over 85 percent indicated on questionnaires the opinion that this was a good method for teaching the beginning reading skill. More than 80 percent thought that the instruction they received was helpful, and about the same number felt that the instruction was important for their children. About 70 percent said that they would like more help of this kind, and more than 75 percent stated an intention to continue practicing the beginning reading activities.

Reactions of Parents Not in the Research Project

Several thousand guidebooks were sold to persons not in either of the research groups. Some of these persons were within viewing range of KRMA-TV and could have seen the programs, while a large number were outside the Denver area. Questionnaires were sent to all guidebook purchasers, and more than one-fourth of the questionnaires were returned.

Of the persons who returned the completed questionnaires, well over half were college graduates, and about 60 percent were in business or the professions. More than 87 percent expected their children to be graduated from college. A high regard for education is evident in this group, whose members would be expected to show interest in the beginning reading activities. At the same time, however, sharp criticism of any method not showing promise could be expected of them.

All guidebook purchasers who returned the questionnaire had at least one child, and over half had a child of preschool age. About 37 percent had children at the lower elementary age (five to seven years). Over three-fourths of these people tried the beginning reading activities with a child, and about the same number found the instruction helpful to the child. About 70 percent said that their children were interested in the activities. At the time they completed the questionnaire, they had gone through about 8 of the 16 lessons in the guidebook; more than half of them indicated an intention to continue with the activities. Fewer than 16 percent felt that the guidebook could be improved in any way. Overall, then, this group reacted favorably to the guidebook and the activities it suggested. For the most part, this attitude was based on actual trial of the activities with young children.

Summary and Conclusions

This study appears to indicate that preschool children can be taught certain basic skills of beginning reading, provided they are about four and one-half years of age or older. The key word here is "taught." In this study, it appeared that the amount the child learned depended directly on the amount that someone practiced the beginning reading activities with him. Further, the minimum amount of practice established as necessary was 30 minutes per week. Statistically significant gains in achievement, as measured by the evaluative instruments, were made by those who practiced 30 minutes or more per week.

A great majority of parents in the project indicated a favorable attitude toward the beginning reading activities and felt that these activities were helpful to their children.

Reading to the child was also found to have a significant effect whether or not the child was in one of the groups which practiced the beginning reading activities. Many parents in the control group, in fact, read to their children and produced an increase in test scores. However, the best performance on the test was by children who had both practiced the beginning reading activities more than 30 minutes a week and had been read to more than 60 minutes a week. It appears, then, that reading to the child should be recommended in connection with the present beginning reading activities.

Most parents who tried the activities felt that they were important and that the method was good.

Many guidebooks were sold to parents not in the project. These purchasers gave a very favorable evaluation of the book and the activities suggested.

The results obtained appear to indicate that parents can help prepare their children for reading, provided the children have sufficient mental maturity. Significant accomplishment, given sufficient mental maturity, depends primarily upon practicing the specified activities with the child.

KINDERGARTEN READING STUDY

A parallel study investigated the effectiveness of beginning the teaching of reading in kindergarten. The longitudinal effects as well as the initial results were examined. The progress of the children in the study was followed from the kindergarten through the fifth grade.

The population sample consisted of approximately 4,000 pupils who were randomly assigned by school to comparable control and experimental groups for kindergarten instruction. The kindergarten instruction of the control and experimental group was similar except for one major difference. The children in the experimental kindergarten groups were given instruction in the beginning reading activities for 20 minutes a day. The children in the control group followed the regular kindergarten program which was quite typical of those in many other parts of the country. The experimental kindergarten children received planned, sequential instruction in beginning reading, while the control kindergarten children had activities which incidentally developed reading readiness.

When the children in the study entered the first grade, the experimental and control groups were in turn divided into two groups. This division provided four first grade groups:

Group 1 The Control Group
  Regular programs in kindergarten
  Regular programs in the first and later grades
Group 2 The Delayed-Experimental Group
  Regular program in kindergarten
  Experimental program in the first grade
  Adjusted program in the first and later grades
Group 3 The Short-term Experimental Group
  Experimental program in kindergarten
  Regular program in the first and later grades
Group 4 The Experimental Group
  Experimental program in kindergarten
  Adjusted program in the first and later grades

Group 1 provided a useful base against which to compare other groups. Group 2 permitted a comparison between groups who received the same instruction introduced at different times. Group 3 made possible the assessment of the effect of introducing reading in kindergarten when a regular reading program was provided in the first and following grades. Group 4 followed an experimental program in kindergarten and a program in first grade adjusted to be consistent in approach with the kindergarten program and accelerated to take advantage of gains made in kindergarten. All groups had the same amount of reading instruction.

The regular reading program referred to in previous matter was that in use prior to the study. It was the reading program detailed in the Denver Public School Reading Guide (8) and was similar to those programs suggested in teachers' manuals of most basal texts. The adjusted program had two characteristics: 1) it was modified to continue use of the experimental technique with adopted basal readers and 2) it provided for their use at an accelerated pace. Both the experimental and regular reading programs were supplemented by extensive use of library books.

Throughout the study, the principal statistical technique was analysis of variance: covariance technique. The primary variable considered was the time of beginning reading; other variables were mental age, chronological age, sex, IQ, and family characteristics. These latter variables were also used as covariates.

Comparisons were made on the criterion variable (reading achievement) between experimental groups and combinations of groups. Effects of other variables were studied in the same way. Analysis of variance also allowed computation of the interaction between variables. A separate analysis of this type was made with mental age, chronological age, sex, IQ, and family characteristics, each used as the independent variable. In every case, attention was given to the interaction of the treatment variable (time of beginning reading) with the other variables in determining the effect of the criterion variable (reading achievement, and the like).

Findings

Ten findings resulted:

1. Beginning reading skills can be taught quite effectively to large numbers of typical kindergarten pupils. Specifically, public school kindergarten children were able to identify words by using together the beginning sound and context. The pupils also learned phonic elements such as letter names, letter forms, and letter-sound associations.

2. The permanence of gains made as a result of being taught beginning reading in the kindergarten depended upon subsequent instruction. Adjustments in the educational program which followed the teaching of kindergarten beginning reading were necessary if the initial gains were to be maintained. Optimum reading achievement was obtained by boys and girls who received the experimental beginning reading instruction in kindergarten and who had an adjusted reading program in later grades. Such adjustment was necessary for the measurable advantages of early reading instruction to be preserved beyond the second grade. When the advantages of an early start in reading were followed up, statistically significant gains in reading achievement persisted throughout the entire study.

3. The gains from the experimental program were evident in both reading comprehension and reading vocabulary. When the reading achievement of the groups in the study was analyzed, it was noted that the accelerated kindergarten beginning reading group had significantly higher levels of reading comprehension than any of the other groups. They had the most effective reading vocabularies of all groups studied and were most able to read with understanding.

4. The results showed that the accelerated kindergarten beginning reading group had significantly higher reading rates: they read with greater speed than any of the other groups when tested at the end of third grade. When evaluated in the fifth grade, their reading speed was equalled only by the other accelerated group.

5. Acceleration or adjustment of the reading program was also an effective means of improving reading achievement. At the end of the study, those boys and girls who had an adjusted or stepped-up program of reading instruction following their use of the experimental instruction in the first grade, rather than in the kindergarten, occupied the second most favorable position in terms of reading achievement.

6. Beginning the teaching of reading in the kindergarten influenced

achievement in other areas where success was dependent upon reading proficiency. This relationship was noted in the areas of word study skills, language, and the social studies.

7. All groups in the study seemed to profit from the additional emphasis on reading. The number of books read independently by all groups was quite impressive. During the first four grades of the investigation, the early kindergarten reading and the accelerated reading groups had the highest percentages of children reading the greatest number of books.

8. The experimental instruction used in the study, i.e., the kindergarten program and the adjusted program used in later grades, proved to be more effective than the regular reading program with which it was compared.

9. No evidence was found that the experimental early instruction in beginning reading affected visual acuity, created problems of school adjustment, or caused dislike for reading. No statistically significant differences existed between groups in these areas.

10. It has been shown that through educational innovation a large urban public school system can significantly upgrade the reading achievement of boys and girls.

Conclusions

Research has established that boys and girls can be taught to read at earlier ages than is generally the case. This fact is commonly recognized by reading authorities. That most children are not taught to read before the age of six years and six months may be attributed to two factors: tradition and fear of harmful results.

Tradition

The traditional influences have been mentioned earlier. They consist of the older research, such as that of Morphett and Washburne (24) and others which suggested a mental age required for reading. When this age was cited, it was taken out of context. It was mentioned independently, and little attention was paid to the nature of the instructional methods and materials being used at the time. Nevertheless, because that beginning mental age coincided with entry into first grade, it came to be widely accepted in this country and the tradition has been reinforced by the reluctance of kindergarten authorities to actively question it.

The influence of certain movements during recent decades has tended to assign kindergartens the responsibility for promoting children's social and emotional growth through informal play experiences. In the intellectual areas, the kindergarten has come to be given a readiness function.

Results of several investigations (*15, 20, 25, 26*) tended to show the efficiency with which these tasks were accomplished in the kindergarten. In the process, however, a tradition was being established. Two worthwhile objectives tended to become dominant: fostering physical development through play experiences and developing social and language skills by means of informal activities. The kindergarten came to contribute little to mental or academic development beyond a not-too-clearly defined concept of "readiness."

Thus, over a period of years, the kindergarten came to be a place where certain things were done and others were not attempted. Recently, when traditional roles have been challenged and introduction of more organized substantive content proposed, change has been resisted because it runs counter to traditional child-growth concepts and because harmful results were feared.

In relation to these objections, there needs to be considered the effect of changing conditions. New insights into the processes of child growth and development are constantly being discovered. The environment of children (and of adults as well) is changing rapidly. Differences of opinion exist among specialists in the field, and yet the positions of all specialists take into account marked variations or a high degree of flexibility in the patterns of child growth and development. In addition to these considerations, the present study has cast some doubt on possible harmful effects resulting from beginning the teaching of reading in the kindergarten.

Findings Concerning Possible Harmful Effects

The results of this investigation were most reassuring concerning potential harm which may result from early reading instruction. No evidence has been found which would substantiate such fears as have been expressed. The concern that the experimental early reading might produce visual defects has not been substantiated. Nor have any grounds been found to support the fear that organized beginning reading instruction in the kindergarten produced harmful social or psychological results. Instead, the evidence showed that the kindergarten beginning reading instruction was retained. Further, it had a measurable, positive, continuing effect. The achievement of the children taught reading in the kindergarten, when built upon in succeeding grades, was significantly higher than that of their peers whose introduction to reading was delayed until the first grade. The former were further ahead after five years than they would have been had reading been taught to them at the later traditional age.

Those who desire further evidence concerning this area should be encouraged to conduct additional studies; if the conclusions are viewed only as "straws in the wind," the conclusions are reassuring. The results suggest that other similar research can and should be carried on with much less trepidation about harming children. Undoubtedly, the potential dangers exist, but the experimental methodology used has shown that harm can be avoided. The possible hazards should be kept in mind, but they do not constitute an excuse for opposing change or for justifying inaction. Little educational progress will be made if doubts and questions operate to prevent efforts to improve current practices.

This study has shown that with appropriate methods and materials of instruction beginning reading can be taught successfully in the kindergarten without harmful effects. To a great extent this is a confirmation of the fact that the mental age required for beginning to read is greatly influenced by the instructional methods and materials employed. Viewed in this way it becomes, as psychologists suggest, a matter of intent and a test of organizing skill.

A surprising and perhaps the most important aspect of the total study is the finding that most average youngsters in a large city public school system can profit from beginning to read in the kindergarten. It long has been recognized that some youngsters had learned to read before entering school. Generally, in this country it was thought that such attainment was possible only by precocious, gifted children having high socioeconomic backgrounds—this, in spite of the fact that children in some countries begin to read at age five. Recent reports by Durkin (11) have also cast doubt upon this assumption. Many of her early readers came from blue-collar families—some having IQs as low as 91.

Somewhat similarly, the children in this study have a wide range of abilities and representative background as found in large urban schools. Elaborate screening or readiness testing was not used. It was felt that the best screening device was the actual beginning reading instruction. Thus, all the children were given the opportunity to begin to learn to read at an early age, and most succeeded in varying degrees. The key seemed to be the opportunity—a chance to begin reading through appropriate, systematic, well-organized instruction.

Other Supporting Evidence

If appropriate environmental stimulation can nurture and spur the development of certain abilities, inappropriate conditions can delay their emergence. It has long been recognized that a general relationship exists between learning and environment. As Bruner (4) states, "It is not surprising in light of this that early opportunities for development have loomed so large in our recent understanding of human mental growth.

The importance of early experience is only dimly sensed today. The experience from animal studies indicates that virtually irreversible deficits can be produced in mammals by depriving them of opportunities that challenge their nascent capacities."

A similar conclusion, based upon research on both animals and humans, has been stated by Deutsch (9). However, until recently, educators have not been fully aware of the exciting possibilities for nurturing intellectual growth through early educational stimulation.

Lately, there has been increasing support for the position that environmental stimuli can accelerate readiness. As Bruner (4) writes, "The idea of readiness is a mischievous half-truth. It is a half-truth largely because it turns out that one teaches readiness or provides opportunities for its nurture; one does not simply wait for it. Readiness, in these terms, consists of mastery of those simple skills that permit one to teach higher skills."

At present, many educational psychologists and theorists are exploring the effect of environment upon learning. They are striving to determine the extent to which early and continuous, structured stimulation of children increases learning of all kinds: cognitive, aesthetic, motor, and affective. Current research reports and contemporary articles in professional journals suggest numerous possibilities for increasing the performance level of children. Equally important, it seems likely that this worthwhile goal can be accomplished without harmful pressure. Indeed, it appears that children naturally welcome and respond to appropriate, stimulating challenges with which they can cope successfully.

The findings of this investigation also tend to support the desirability of a stimulating environment. They indicate that early sequentially structured stimulation results in high levels of symbolic learning. To the extent that this is so, school systems need to reexamine their kindergarten curriculum to determine its adequacy in line with emerging theory.

Other recent investigations support the findings of the Denver study. Moore (23) reports that after five years of teaching two-, three-, and four-year-olds to read, no signs of physical or psychological strain have been detected by pediatricians and psychologists.

Anderson (2) found that children of varied mental abilities, as young as four years and four months, benefited from early, planned reading instruction. McManus (21), replicating a Denver study of The Effectiveness of Parents Preparing Their Children for Reading, and Brzeinski and Hayman (5) reaffirmed the value of parents' helping their children learn to read at an early age. Hillerich (17), describing a study involving the teaching of beginning reading skills, found that children who were taught formal beginning reading in the kindergarten were better readers at the end of first grade than children who had not had such training.

Schoephoerster and others (27), reporting a recent study, found that a formal readiness program including pupil use of a workbook helped children of all ability levels more than did an informal readiness program without pupil use of workbooks. In regard to such kindergarten instruction's creating frustration, emotional problems, or a permanent dislike for reading, Schoephoerster states that not one incident occurred or one piece of evidence appeared which would lend credence to such contentions.

Additional support for the position that early reading instruction does not cause visual defects is found in a recent report by Shaw (29), who states that "From a purely physical point of view, since most normal children can focus and accommodate at the age of twelve months, children's eyes are efficient enough for them to be taught to read at twelve months of age. . . . If a child has normal eyes, is in good health, and has good intelligence, he can read at an early age."

Thus, the evidence from different sources suggests that early reading need not adversely affect children's vision. Obviously, any defects which may normally exist should be detected as quickly as possible and corrected so that optimum reading achievement is possible.

No doubt, the potential for good or evil is inherent in early reading instruction, as it is in most education. In the past, perhaps, too much attention has been directed to the potential dangers and too little to the many beneficial aspects which may result from early reading instruction. An extremely common sense position concerning early reading instruction is that taken by Durrell and Nicholson who point out, "If child interest is one basis for planning preschool or kindergarten programs, it seems that early aspects of reading and writing should be included for some children. The fact that others may show little interest in these activities may be taken as a clue for extra effort. It is difficult to discover any peculiarity about early abilities related to reading and writing that excludes them from a developmental educational program. While there is objection to forcing the child in language activities, this objection applies equally to all phases of child development and it is assumed that a good teacher will apply only desirable motivations in all of them (13).

Implications

The implications seem clear. School systems need to reevaluate the goals they have established for their kindergartens. Emerging psychological theory, recent research evidence, and the findings of the present study suggest that children profit from early educational stimulation. Children today appear to possess a greater aptitude for learning as a result of changes which have occurred in their environments. Improvements have been made in the methods and materials of instruction. It seems reasonable to suggest that school teachers and administrators should reconsider the role of the kindergarten.

The Denver study was limited to the development of beginning reading skills in the kindergarten. It is quite likely that other systems may prefer to explore the possibility of introducing other simple language, writing, science, or number skills, to name but a few possibilities; or it may well be that other school districts may wish to test other suitable beginning reading approaches in the kindergarten. It is entirely possible that through continuing exploration a better developmental program than that adopted for the purposes of the present study could be developed. Actually, the important task is to determine what is appropriate for kindergarten boys and girls in the conditions of the world today. This study was a pioneering venture in many ways. Much remains to be discovered. For example, what environmental conditions produce increased cognitive learning? How can the optimum time be determined for introducing these learnings to each child? What are the ways by which maximum reinforcement can be given to skills developed early in a child's school life?

On a very practical level, the awareness of what is possible—that some children may come to school reading and that others can be taught early—should lead every kindergarten teacher to differentiate her instruction so that each child may fully develop his aptitudes. The kindergarten teacher must feel free to teach beginning reading skills to some pupils and to delay systematic instruction for others. In this way, the extremes of reading or no reading can be avoided.

Obviously, no single kindergarten curriculum is suitable for all pupils. Generally, in the past, the practice has been to hold back those who might reasonably progress faster. A flexible kindergarten pattern is required which permits each pupil to achieve at his own rate.

Change has been occurring at a phenomenal rate in most areas of education. Presently, its influence is being felt in the kindergarten. School administrators have a responsibility to lead in the reappraisal of what constitutes appropriate kindergarten education. Their efforts may be aided by the findings of the present study and the use of other current research reports. Teachers, confused by conflicting opinions of those holding various positions, would do well to inaugurate informal research within their classrooms in order to determine what is possible with the boys and girls they teach. In this way, improvements in kindergarten education can be made—improvements which will preserve long-recognized values, while adding new dimensions required by the conditions of the world today. Through such efforts and through carefully planned research, the emerging role of the kindergarten may be defined.

REFERENCES

1. Almy, Millie. *Children's Experiences Prior to First Grade and Success in Beginning Reading.* New York: Bureau of Publication, Teachers College, Columbia University, 1949.
2. Anderson, Dorothy M. "A Study to Determine if Children Need a Mental Age of Six Years and Six Months to Learn to Identify Strange Printed Word Forms When They Are Taught to Use Oral Context and the Initial Sound of the Word," unpublished doctoral dissertation, Colorado State College, 1960.
3. Bruner, Jerome S. "Education as Social Invention," *Saturday Review,* February 19, 1966, 70.
4'. Bruner, Jerome S. "Education as Social Invention," *Saturday Review,* February 19, 1966, 72.
5. Brzeinski, Joseph E., and John L. Hyman, Jr. *The Effectiveness of Parents Helping Their Preschool Children to Begin Reading.* Denver: Denver Public Schools, 1962.
6. Committee of Reading. *Studies in Reading,* publication of the Scottish Council for Research in Education. London: University of London Press, 1950. *Educational Journal,* 45 (September 1951-May 1952).
7. Denver Public Schools. "The Effectiveness of Teaching Reading in Kindergarten," Multilithed, 1960.
8. *Denver Public Schools Reading Guide,* for use in elementary schools. Denver Public Schools, 1948.
9. Deutsch, Martin. *Teachers College Record,* January 1966, 260.
10. Drews, Elizabeth M., and John E. Teehan. "Parental Attitudes and Academic Achievement," *Journal of Clinical Psychology,* 13 (October 1957), 328-332.
11. Durkin, Dolores. "A Study of Children Who Learned to Read Prior to First Grade," *California Journal of Educational Research,* 10 (May 1959), 80.
12. Durkin, Dolores. "Children Who Read before Grade One," *Reading Teacher,* 14 (January 1961).
13. Durrel, Donald, and Alice Nicholson. "Preschool and Kindergarten Experience," *Sixtieth Yearbook of the National Society for the Study of Education, Development in and through Reading.* Bloomington: Public School Publishing Company, 1961, 257.
14. Eames, Thomas H. "Physical Factors in Reading," *Reading Teacher,* 15 (May 1962).
15. Fast, Irene. "Kindergarten Training and Grade 1 Reading," *Journal of Educational Psychology,* 48 (January 1957), 53-57.

16. Gates, Arthur I. *The Improvement of Reading*. New York: Macmillan, 1954.
17. Hillerich, Robert L. *Elementary School Journal*, March 1965, 313.
18. Hollingshead, August B. "Two Factor Index of Social Position." Mimeographed, 1957.
19. Kansler, Donald H. "Aspiration Level as a Determinant of Performance," *Journal of Personality*, 27 (May 1959), 346-351.
20. McLatchy, Josephine. *Attendance at Kindergarten and Progress in the Primary Grades*. Columbus: Ohio State University, 1928.
21. McManus, Anastasia. "The Denver Prereading Project Conducted by WENH-TV," *Reading Teacher*, 18 (October 1964), 22.
22. Monroe, Marion, and Bertie Backus. *Remedial Reading: A Monograph in Character Education*. Boston: Houghton Mifflin, 1937.
23. Moore, Omar K. "Orthographic Symbols and the Preschool Child—A New Approach," unpublished paper, Yale University, 1959.
24. Morphett, Mable, and Carleton Washburne. "When Should Children Begin to Read?" *Elementary School Journal*, 31 (March 1931), 496-503.
25. Morrison, J. Cayce. "Influence of Kindergarten on the Age-Grade Progress of Children Entering School under Six Years of Age: Abstract," *Role of Research in Educational Progress*. American Educational Research Association, 1937, 19-21.
26. Pratt, Willis E. "A Study of the Differences in the Prediction of Reading Success of Kindergarten and Non-Kindergarten Children," *Journal of Educational Research*, 42 (March 1949), 525-533.
27. Schoephoerster, Hugh, Richard Barnhart, and Walter M. Loomer. "The Teaching of Prereading Skills in Kindergarten," *Reading Teacher*, 19 (February 1966), 353-357.
28. Serot, Naomi M., and Richard C. Teevan. "Perception of Parent-Child Relationship and Its Relationship to Child Adjustment," *Child Development*, 32 (June 1961), 373-378.
29. Shaw, Jules H. "Vision and Seeing Skills of Preschool Children," *Reading Teacher*, 18 (October 1964), 35.
30. Vernon, M. D. *Backwardness in Reading*. Cambridge: University Press, 1958.
31. Wilson, Frank T. "Reading Progress in Kindergarten and Primary Grades," *Elementary School Journal*, February 1938.

How Parents are Teaching Their Preschoolers to Read

Lee Mountain

FIVE . . . FOUR . . . THREE . . . TWO . . . Perhaps this countdown makes you think of a launching from Cape Kennedy. Or perhaps it makes you think of an even more important kind of launching—launching your child into reading. Many a mother has discovered that she can help her child start to read at the age of five . . . four . . . three . . . two.

The idea of teaching the preschooler to read has been gaining popularity since the early 1960s. At the Institute for the Achievement of Human Potential in Philadelphia, Dolman (*4*) has claimed to have helped hundreds of parents teach their babies to read. Durkin (*5*) has indicated that the children she studied who learned to read before entering school maintained their advantage in school. The Denver Study showed long term benefits with no adverse side effects for children who started to read at the age of five (*2*). Educators who work with two- to four-year-olds have reported success in reading instruction with television teaching (*8*), the talking typewriter (*10*), programed instruction (*6*), and special nursery school materials (*9*). These methods, however, are somewhat dependent upon complicated equipment, so they are not ideal for home use by a parent.

Parents want reading instruction materials that are economical and easy to use. Parents also want to teach their preschoolers by a method that will tie in well with whatever approach the children will meet in first grade. However, there is a shortage of simple, economical, how-to-teach information for parents of children who are ready to start reading at early ages (3). This shortage led me to work on developing some approaches that a parent could use to give his preschooler a headstart on reading.

For the past four years, some of my graduate students at the Rutgers University Reading Center have been working with me on methods and materials for teaching their own sons and daughters to read. We have tried simplifying some first grade methods for use at the preschool level (1, 7). We have also tried using some economical commercial materials with two- to five-year-olds (11, 12). We are presently working on other approaches.

The simplest and most economical method we have developed so far employs three materials: 1) word cards, 2) stories written by the parent, and 3) phonics games. With these materials, perhaps you and your child can have as much fun and success as the parents and children who used them at Rutgers University. If you want to try our approach, here is how you can offer your preschooler a headstart on reading.

WORD CARDS

For making word cards you need some unlined three-by-five cards and a black crayon or magic marker. Print the word *Mommy* on one of the cards, using a capital for the first letter only. Then staple strings to the card so that you can hang it around your neck. But before you put on your *Mommy* card, say to your child, "What do you call me?" Or ask another question that will get the response *Mommy*. Then say, "Yes, I am Mommy, and this is the word *Mommy*," as you put the card around your neck. Have your child look at the word, touch the card, and repeat *Mommy* after you.

Sometimes the child catches on so quickly that you never get a chance to wear the *Mommy* card. One graduate student reported this experience in teaching the word *Mommy* to her three-year-old son.

> This afternoon I read Mike's favorite book to him. Then I asked him if he would like to learn to read. He wanted to begin at once. As soon as I presented the *Mommy* card, he took it from me, walked away, and put it on his toy chest. Later, I rescued my card from his baby sister who was nibbling an edge of it. The next day I asked him to read the word on the card. He took one look and said, "Mommy." Later I printed *Mommy* on a smaller card in red ink. When I held it up, he said "Mommy." Wow!

Another graduate student reported a very different experience with her three-year-old daughter:

ILLUSTRATION 1

After two weeks of no success with the word *Mommy*, I switched my teaching tactics. I started playing phonics games with Amy. We would take turns thinking of words that started with the same sound. Then I showed her the letter *M* to match the sound *mmmmmmm*. Once she could match a few letters and sounds, everything seemed to fall into place. She learned *Mommy* easily, and she soon picked up a number of other words.

If you find yourself getting nowhere on the teaching of *Mommy* after a week or two of one-minute daily sessions, you might want to try phonics games instead. Or you might want to wait a while before going ahead with reading instruction. Since you have taught your child to talk and to use the toilet, you know from experience that your teaching doesn't always "take" on the first few tries. But if your teaching does "take," you should soon remove the string from your *Mommy* card, stand it up on the table where your child will see it at each meal, and review it frequently.

Make a *Daddy* card for your husband. But before he starts wearing it, prepare your child for learning the word *Daddy*. Point out that you and your husband look different and that the words *Mommy* and *Daddy* look different, too.

Directing your child's attention to similarities is also helpful. For example, when introducing the *Daddy* card, one mother pointed out to her four-year-old, "The letter *D* has a fat tummy, and so does Daddy."

When your husband hangs the card around his neck, he should say, "This is the word *Daddy*." Have your child look at the card and repeat *Daddy*. Of course, both you and your husband will show how pleased you are when your child begins to learn the word. After he seems to know it, remove the string, put it on the table with the *Mommy* card, and review it frequently.

A child who has been able to learn the words *Mommy* and *Daddy* will have no trouble learning to read his own name. To teach your child to read his name, use a hand mirror with a card taped on it. Print his name on the card, using a capital for the first letter only. (Your child can't wear his name card like a necklace because he would then see the word upside down.) Hand him the mirror and say something to this effect: "You can see yourself in the mirror, and you see your name on the card." Have him point to the card and read his name. When your child no longer needs the mirror for a clue, review his name from the card alone. Label many of his belongings with his name and have him practice reading his name on his toys, clothes, and furniture.

After you have taught your child to read three nouns—*Mommy, Daddy,* and his own name—you need to introduce a verb so that he can read a few sentences. The verb *kisses* is a good one to start with since it has meaning and significance for a preschooler. Also it is handy for building sentences, such as *Daddy kisses Mommy.*

One of my graduate students reported instant success with this presentation of the word *kisses.*

> After I showed Stephen the *kisses* card and told him what it said, I scooped him up and planted millions of kisses on his cheeks, nose, eyes, ears, and neck. He never again had to be told what that word card said.

I observed that many two- and three-year-olds love to "practice" by rereading the words they already know. But some four- and five-year-olds are so eager to learn a lot of words rapidly that they need extra encouragement to practice the words they are learning.

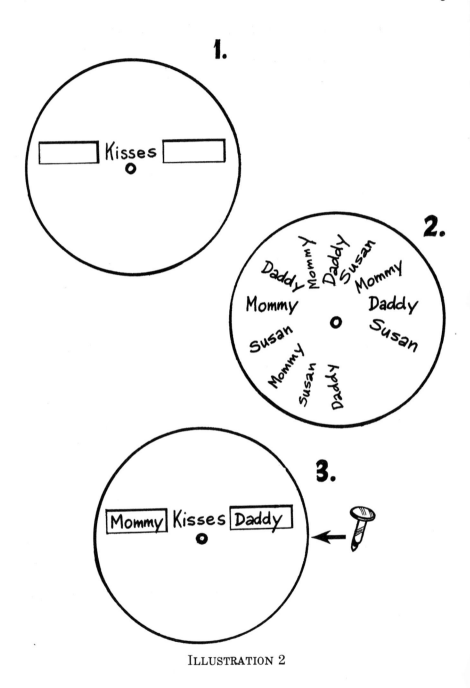

ILLUSTRATION 2

One mother of a five-year-old reported that her daughter, Susan, learned *Mommy, Daddy,* her own name, and *kisses* during her first ten-minute lesson. Susan then asked for more words. Because the mother wanted to provide some practice on the first four words, she and Susan constructed a sentence wheel with two circles of paper and a pronged clip.

When a preschooler knows his first four words and can read them in sentences with expression and comprehension, it is time to ask him what words he would like to learn next. Some preschoolers want more proper names, such as *Santa* and *Fido.* Others want action verbs like *jump* and *swim.* Your preschooler will have his own ideas about which words he wants in his early reading vocabulary. That is why you are the best author of reading material for your preschool child. You know which words your child wants to learn. You can teach him those words on word cards, and you can then write those words into stories for him to read.

STORIES WRITTEN BY THE PARENT

My graduate students found that they needed very few words to write stories about the everyday happenings in the lives of their children. Here, for example, is a four-sentence story told with only six different words: Jim hit Paul. Paul cried. Grandpa spanked Jim. Jim cried. While this story has something resembling a plot, such a characteristic is not really the sine qua non of a story for the typical three-year-old reader. My graduate students found that their three-year-olds were perfectly happy with plotless stories as long as the stories were about themselves. Parents turned out dozens of homemade storybooks about their children. Typical pages are illustrated below.

Mark's "book" is just a piece of paper folded in half. To make Kathy's "book," her father stapled together a few sheets of looseleaf notebook paper on which he had printed sentences and pasted snapshots. If you can draw even a stick figure, your child will love having you illustrate the books you write for him. But if drawing is not your forte, snapshots seem to be equally acceptable as illustrations for homemade books.

Of necessity, the typical parent-written story abounds in two types of words: 1) names of friends and relatives and 2) action verbs. These are the types of words that preschoolers are most interested in learning since these words are connected with their favorite people and activities.

To teach your child the names he wants to read, use the same word-card procedures you employed when teaching *Mommy* and *Daddy.* Capitalize each name, but use lower case printing for the other letters. Usually names of brothers, sisters, and playmates can be learned easily,

ILLUSTRATION 3

provided the words in print do not closely resemble one another. For example, because *Danny* can be confused with *Daddy,* it may be wise to avoid presenting *Danny* soon after *Daddy.* Try to teach names that look fairly different from one another, and teach only one new name at a time. Name card necklaces may be worn by sisters and brothers. Sometimes a snapshot on the name card helps your child learn to read the name of a relative.

To review the name cards, use activities such as having your child set up name cards at the table. Play school, letting your child pretend to call the roll from name cards of his friends. Print the names he knows on envelopes, and have him play mailman or delivery boy. Be careful to proceed at your child's own pace. One new name each week is plenty for some children. Others want to make a name card telephone directory by adding a new name every day.

You can teach the second type of word—the action verb—in much

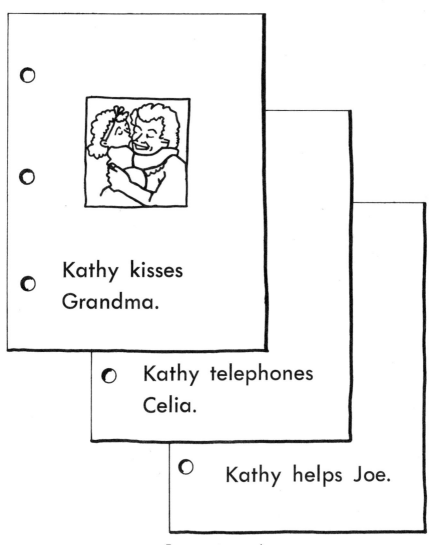

ILLUSTRATION 4

the same way that you taught *kisses*. Just demonstrate and talk about the action, and make sure your child uses the word orally with ease. To review action words, hold up one card at a time and have your child perform the action.

Most two- and three-year-olds appear to be content reading books that contain *only* nouns and verbs, but some four- and five-year-olds want to move beyond noun and verb stories. They want to learn to read words like *up, under, is, will, he, I, so,* and *but.* Such words are not so concrete and, therefore, not so easy to teach as nouns and action verbs. They are learned best through a combination of repetition and phonics. You can provide many repetitions of these words in the stories you write. And you can play phonics games with your child to build his awareness of sounds and letters so that he can eventually start to apply his knowledge of phonics to words that are hard for him to learn to read.

PHONICS GAMES

You can start to play sound games with your child at the same time that you start teaching him to recognize the word *Mommy.* You might say, "I'm thinking of a word that starts with the sound *mmmm.* Guess what it is." If your child doesn't understand what you want, tell him that *MMMMMommy* starts with the sound *mmmm.* Or you might tell your child, "I see two things in the yard that begin (or end) with the sound *mmmmm.* What are they?" Another approach would be to ask your child, "What sound do you hear at the beginning of the words *saw, see,* and *Sue?"*

These games will help your child become aware of sounds. For reading he needs to connect a sound with a letter. So show him the *Mommy* card again, point to the capital *M,* and say, "This letter stands for the sound *mmmmm.* The word *Mommy* starts with *mmmmm."* Have him repeat *mmmmm* after you. After he has made the connection between the sound *mmmmm* and the letter *M,* use the same procedure to teach the sounds of other letters.

One mother that I worked with developed an interesting "kitchen approach" to phonics. She decided that the way to her child's brain was through his stomach. So she baked batch after batch of alphabet cookies. If he knew the sound, he could eat the letter. He became proficient at phonics very rapidly.

Some commercial games are handy for phonics instruction. With *Scrabble for Juniors* you can give your child practice in recognizing and matching letters and producing their sounds.

Once your child knows a few letters and sounds, he can profit from playing *Word Roll.* In this game your child throws a pair of dice such as those shown in the following illustration and then attempts to sound out the word on the upper faces.

Most of my graduate students used phonics games along with word cards and homemade storybooks when teaching their children to read. After you have taught your child his first few words, you will find yourself using all three materials—word cards, stories you have written, and phonics games—in your at-home teaching session.

ILLUSTRATION 5

With phonics games, as with the other teaching materials, you should go only as far as your child wants to go. If he enjoys phonics games, play them frequently. If sounds and letters seem too abstract for him, stop, wait a few months, and try again.

With just these three simple materials—word cards, homemade books, and phonics games—many parents have been able to help their pre-schoolers start to read. Maybe you can do as much for your child when he is five . . . four . . . three . . . two. If you decide to try, here's wishing you, "Happy teaching!"

References

1. Ashton-Warner, Sylvia. *Teacher.* New York: Simon and Schuster, 1963.
2. Brzeinski, J. "Beginning Reading in Denver," *Reading Teacher,* 18 (1964), 16-21.
3. Della-Piana, G., R. F. Stahmann, and J. E. Allen. "Parents and Reading Achievement: A Review of Research," *Elementary English,* 45 (1968), 190-200.
4. Doman, Glenn. *How to Teach Your Baby to Read.* New York: Random House, 1964.
5. Durkin, Dolores. *Children Who Read Early: Two Longitudinal Studies.* New York: Teachers College Press, Columbia University, 1966, 133.
6. Fowler, W. "A Study of Process and Method in Three-Year-Old Twins and Triplets Learning to Read," *Genetic Psychology Monograph,* 72 (1965), 3-89.
7. Harris, Albert J. *How to Increase Reading Ability.* New York: David McKay, 1961.
8. Harvey, Neil. "Once It Was Believed," *Reading Newsreport,* 3 (November 1968), 25.
9. Montessori, M. *The Montessori Method.* Cambridge: Robert Bentley, 1964.
10. Moore, O., and A. Anderson. *The Response Environment Project Current Theory and Practice.* Chicago: Aldine, 1967.
11. *Scrabble for Juniors.* New York: Selchow and Righter, 1958.
12. *Word Roll Game.* Indianapolis: Teaching Aids, 1969.

What Parents Should Know about Reading Comprehension

James F. Kerfoot

AN ACTIVE PARENTAL interest in education has always been an important factor in a child's success. Actively interested parents who understand the reading process can do much to facilitate their children's achievements. However, actively interested parents who lack basic understandings can create conditions which strongly bias against their children's growth in reading. What should parents know about reading comprehension? It is not easy to determine what *teachers* should know about comprehension. Presumably parents will not need to know as much, or perhaps parents should simply view comprehension from a different perspective.

PARENTS SHOULD UNDERSTAND THAT THE PURPOSE FOR READING IS COMPREHENSION

Parents should recognize that word calling is not reading and that until a meaningful communication is taking place between the author and the reader, there is no comprehension—there is no reading, by any acceptable definition of that process.

In an article on the nature of reading comprehension, Cleland (2) cited several definitions of reading including his own in which he viewed reading as "establishment of rapport with an author." Other definitions include "The goal of all reading is a comprehension of meaning" (3) and "Comprehension is just a big blanket term that covers a whole area of thought getting processes in reading" (*5*). Bond and Wagner (*1*) wrote that "Reading is the process of acquiring an author's meaning and of interpreting, evaluating, and reflecting upon that meaning." Reading is thus defined by the great majority of writers in some meaning-emphasis terms. While recognizing the necessity for decoding skill as a means, it is inescapable to concede that the purpose for reading is comprehension.

PARENTS SHOULD RECOGNIZE THAT THERE ARE DIFFERENT TYPES OF COMPREHENSION

Simple understanding of an author's message has been called literal comprehension. A child will grow in reading fluency until he is able to obtain from the printed page the same completeness of meaning he would have received if he had listened to the passage spoken to him.

Literal comprehension is most efficiently achieved when attention is directed to the meanings residing in units of different length and structure. At the word level, children will learn the meanings of many different words. Further, a particular word may have a number of meanings to which children must respond. Other unit levels which require special attention include the phrase, the sentence, the paragraph, and the total selection. Each has its own unique structure and consequent comprehension problems.

In addition to literal comprehension, it must be understood that there are a number of purposes for which a child may read which require some manipulation of the ideas in the selection. Inferences may be drawn; evaluations may be made; reorganization of the selection may take place for particular purposes. The reader will be challenged by a variety of conceptual content and a range of purposes which call for different responses to reading material. While the first objective of the comprehension program is to maximize the communication between author and reader at the level of literal comprehension, the second is to provide the reader with an effective range of thinking skills with which to appropriately manipulate the author's ideas in relation to the reader's purposes and his other experiences.

Many would argue that beyond literal comprehension the skills being developed are not reading at all, but thinking. While one would concede that much of the program is concerned with the uses to which reading may be put, it can be easily seen that important thinking skills taught in the reading comprehension program are best developed through reading, though they may in fact not be reading skills. Many classification schemes have been attempted for the reading comprehension skills. Although they are widely disparate in their specific nomenclature, the range of skills encompassed by most classifications is remarkably similar. The numerous thought-getting processes thus identified are discretely evaluated and taught in the reading program.

Parents Should Understand the Factors which Influence Reading Comprehension

Comprehension is affected by decoding skills. Children who fail to derive meaning from reading may fail to do so because attention is intensively focused upon the recognition of words. It is difficult to maintain the meaning of a passage while struggling to identify its several parts. It is essential that the reader develop fluency in word recognition if maximum comprehension is to be attained.

Comprehension is affected by intelligence. If comprehension is to be thought of as a network of thought-getting processes, the upper limits to understanding will be set by the reader's thought-getting abilities. The intellectual capacities of the learner will determine how effectively he will respond to a program emphasizing the high order manipulation of ideas.

Comprehension is affected by experience. It is axiomatic in reading instruction that the reader will "derive from the printed page only in proportion to the experiences which he brings to it," that the experiences provide the meanings. Even with the simplest concepts on which we base communication, there is a world of difference in the imagery of any two people. An author using the simple word "stream" will likely feel confident that his communication with the reader was direct and unambiguous. But no two readers who understand the word "stream" will visualize exactly the same stream. Each will differ in particulars. Each stream will exist in a particular setting, in a particular place, and be quite different from that of another reader or of the author. The meanings obtained from the printed page are so dependent upon the experiences of the reader that it is doubtful whether comprehension as such can really be taught. As Schleich (4) points out, "We can teach certain basic skills on which comprehension and interpretation rely in part. We cannot teach comprehension and interpretation because, as we all know, comprehension and interpretation are based on past as well as present experiences, and the wider and deeper the past experience, the more background the reader has for making judgments, the better will be his comprehension and interpretation. It is a simple maxim, 'the more you bring to a book, the more you will take from it.' Experience and the concepts that relate to it come slowly and cumulatively, and no amount of skills 'teaching' can offset the lack of experience . . . breadth of vocabulary springing from experience."

Comprehension is affected by language development. Comprehension is dependent upon the fluency with which a reader decodes printed symbols into his already mastered oral language patterns. If oral language is inadequate, there will be no fluency. Underlying reading is a spoken language into which written words must be translated. Inadequacy, in language fluency, in general and specialized vocabulary, or in the signal system which we try to represent in reading through punctuation, will limit comprehension.

It should be clear to parents that while a program of specific comprehension skills is being developed, the reader must steadily over a long period of time be brought to higher and higher levels of word recognition, experience, and language facility. Parents can play a vital role in developing experiential and language backgrounds. Parents who provide children with many and varied real and vicarious experiences and expressive opportunities can powerfully influence comprehension growth.

Parents Should Understand that Several Strategies Will Be Used by Teachers to Develop Comprehension

Content will be varied. Significant growth in reading comprehension will be generated by exposing readers to varied content with specialized vocabulary and unique ways of thinking. The form in which information is cast will differ among the content fields. An integrated program of comprehension development will, therefore, require a broad range of content exposures.

Understanding will be developed through preparation for reading. Before a reader is on his own with a selection, he will be prepared for the reading by his teacher. The interest and drive of the learner will be generated as the necessary backgrounds for understanding a selection are developed. Relevant experiences and specialized ways of thinking may be discussed, and the vocabulary to be encountered will be carefully previewed. Through preparation for a selection, the reader can derive greater comprehension since he approaches the task possessing the essential specific background for understanding.

A meaningful setting will aid comprehension development. Among the several methods of teaching reading today, most methods present skills in a meaningful setting. Word recognition is taught in a real context of words in coherent sequences rather than in isolation. Whether word recognition is most readily learned under such conditions, it is certain that children will develop better reading comprehension when the setting in which learning takes place emphasizes meaning.

Comprehension will be developed through listening activities. Listening and reading are closely related language forms. Both require of the learner an accurate literal reception and appropriate relational thinking. A child with word recognition difficulties can continue to grow in thought-getting processes through listening activities while at the same time receiving instruction in word recognition with lower level, less complex material. Listening activities will support and add to the reading comprehension program at all levels and will be frequently used by effective teachers.

Comprehension will be developed by perceptive questioning. The judicious use of questions setting the purposes for reading is the heart of the comprehension program. Teachers will ask readers a variety of questions to deliberately structure an appropriate range of thought patterns. If only questions calling for specific information are asked, readers will become effective fact gatherers and little else. If we wish children to be critical readers, then the questions we ask must elicit critical thinking. If we wish children to draw inferences well, we must ask inferential questions. The carefully selected question is a powerful means for guiding readers toward more effective reading comprehension.

Comprehension will be developed through group interaction. Much use is currently being made of self-instructional procedures for reading instruction. Such procedures have been demonstrated to be of value and have earned an important place in the classroom. Nevertheless, some of the most important outcomes of reading instruction, those aspects of reading comprehension which involve critical interpretation and analysis, may be best developed by the intensive interchange of ideas and the debate possible only in a group setting. Teachers are aware that the development of critical thinking will best occur as the reader's biases and standards are vigorously assailed. A classroom alive with debate is one in which the thought-getting processes are under maximum challenge.

Parents will find in the modern classroom a program rich in its variety of reading material and in which language and experiential backgrounds are steadily developing. Parents will observe children creatively responding to both listening and reading tasks, and they will find teachers carefully preparing children for the difficulties of the selections to be read and setting purposes for reading which will generate greater breadth and depth of understanding. Parents will discover a climate of challenge and interaction in which children are catalyzed to critical analysis and open-mindedness in preparation for a future in which thought and understanding will, hopefully, prevail.

REFERENCES

1. Bond, Guy L., and Eva .Bond Wagner. *Teaching the Child to Read* (3rd ed.). New York: Macmillan, 1960, 4.

2. Cleland, Donald L. "The Nature of Comprehension," *Progress and Promise in Reading Instruction*, Proceedings of 22nd Conference on Reading. Pittsburgh: University of Pittsburgh, 1966, 19, 32.
3. Dechant, Emerald V. *Improving the Teaching of Reading.* Englewood Cliffs, New Jersey: Prentice-Hall, 1964, 353.
4. Schleich, Miriam. "Sequential Reading Skills at the College Level," in J. Allen Figurel (Ed.), *Reading and Inquiry*, Proceedings, 10. Newark, Delaware: International Reading Association, 1965, 39-42.
5. Smith, Nila Banton. *Reading Instruction for Today's Children.* Englewood Cliffs, New Jersey: Prentice-Hall, 1963, 257.

How to Read a Report on Reading in the Popular Press

Lorena A. Anderson

WHEN I FIRST LOOKED at the topic assigned to me—*How to Read a Popular Article On Reading*—I immediately thought, "Oh! They want me to talk about how we add meaning to or delete meaning from what we read as well as from what we hear." The only association or only experience I could apply on the spot to this topic was an experience with a little eight-year-old neighbor. David was a neighborhood youngster. One among many things that alarmed David's mother was his reading and quoting of facts that weren't there, facts that tended to be sensational or morbid. For instance, David would say, "Mother, did you read the headlines today? In Texas 429 men, women, and children were killed in an airplane wreck," or "Mother, did you read where one boy knifed three girls in Ohio," or "Mother, did you read today about a man murdering seven people in California?" And always David would tell about blood, about struggles, about horrors.

Finally, in desperation the mother decided to confront David and ask him if he always believed what he read although she knew he *wasn't* reading what he was reporting. That afternoon, as usual, David came in, saying, "Mother, did you know that 56 airplanes were shot down in Korea?" His mother looked up from her dishes and asked, "David, do you always believe everything you read?" David answered quickly and firmly, "I believe everything I've read and some things I ain't have read."

So, I wondered if this maybe was what the topic was all about—not only believing what we read but also adding our own interpretation. I

decided I'd give you four *wh* question transforms that you, as a reader, might ask yourself as you read any popular article on reading:
1. What background in reading does this author have?
2. What number of people have been involved in this research?
3. What is the cost in dollars and cents of this reading program?
4. What critical and analytical reading skills should I use in reading this article?

Let's look at *wh* question No. 1. In the past 10 to 15 years the popular magazines have been filled with articles concerning reading. Actually, reading has been extolled with black headlines that at times were sensational. It is healthy and wise that so much attention is being given to the teaching of reading by the general public, but it can be unhealthy and unwise if the attention is focused on questionable research and unproved data. It is even worse if the articles promulgate one personality or one technique to the exclusion of all others. Medical men have long had to deal with this problem of what they term "quackery," but it is only in the recent past that reading as a part of the curriculum has been not only a popular lay issue but a controversial lay issue.

It is not uncommon to see write-ups offering help to mother in teaching her two-year-old to read; and mother, particularly if the child is a first, is eager to give the program a try and thus sends for the product and promptly begins. The mother may be lucky and do no harm because the program is good, but her success lies only with luck, not wisdom or good judgment. One good adage to follow then as a layman is "If the reading program is a be all for all, be cautious."

So, with all the attention and space in magazines, newspapers, and pamphlets being given to reading, it perhaps behooves the general public to read carefully themselves and to consider carefully some pertinent facts. The general public might ask first: Why does the writer have the authority to discuss publicly such technical data? What is his background? What are his qualifications?

It is a sad fact of education that some highly publicized reading programs have been developed by nonreading specialists. While these programs may have some valuable aspects, they may be limited because the developer focused on only one of the many important skills necessary for reading.

Sometimes the author of the article is a good writer but an absolute amateur in the field of reading. The writer hears about a *different* reading program; he needs an angle for his writing. He interviews the authority and writes the story to interest his magazine readers, not as a true educator to inform the general public honestly and fairly but as a writer to tell a good story.

The general public needs to find out if the writer is reporting accurately. Is he an active educator, a teacher, a college professor, a reading clinician, or a reading specialist? Then, if he is an educator, what are his qualifications as a researcher and evaluator?

Has the writer written for many publications? Have his writings been accepted by national educational publications? Has this writer completed several research projects? These questions should be used to check the author's educational qualifications.

We can say that the American public in many instances is to blame for the attitudes, the naivety, the gullibility toward all facets of living, including education. If a public can concoct its own image of a president's wife without foundation and decide to accept gossip about one American president and reject the truth about another, then that same public can be expected to be swayed by articles and sensational stories. The book *Why Johnny Can't Read,* for instance, started the biggest onslaught of phonics in reading that this world has ever seen—right or wrong!

We forget that an article or a story could have been written for such a simple reason as to satisfy public demands. Editors want to please, and publishers want to sell. Sometimes we, the public, are merely given what we ask for.

A research report will generally be as honest as the researcher can make it. However, all of us know individuals who become so enthusiastic they cannot be objective in their judgment. The tone of the article, the wording can be clues to credibility. When such phrases as "every child responded 100 percent" or "in two weeks the nonreaders could recognize 320 words" appear in an article, the reader should become wary.

Now for *wh* question No. 2: Besides considering authorship, the reader should peruse carefully the size of the sample on which the writer is basing his research conclusions. Articles are sometimes written by a mother who has worked with her one child. The evaluation of this project must be considered as a project with only one child as a participant.

Sometimes an article concerns a private clinic or school owned by one individual who has developed his own program. This individual cannot make a comparison of reading materials because he uses only his own. In reality, often these programs are not used widely, and other research is not permitted.

A school system will occasionally promote a reading program and, because test scores show improvement, will not experiment with other types of programs. Thus, the school system appears to be saying, "This program is the best on the market; we are endorsing this program."

When a report is written concerning perhaps 50 classrooms with experimental groups and with a research design followed and comparisons made with matching classrooms, then one may say to himself, "I should take a look at this research. The findings might be meaningful and worthwhile."

Sometimes research is carried on with the accelerated student, yet this fact is not made quite clear in the report. Therefore, the statistics appear to be fantastic. Here again, when gains are reported as magnanimous in just a few weeks, a good rule for all of us to follow is to stop, look, and listen carefully. Then stop again, look again, and listen again. On the other hand, a program may be used with the disadvantaged, the slow learner, or youngsters with language problems and be shown as highly successful. These programs may not have any real value for the average reader.

Besides the background of the author of the popular magazine article being of utmost importance and besides the *where*, the *who*, and the *how many* conducting the research being highly important, another vital point that sometimes is misleading to the public is the cost of the reading program to schools. This brings us to *wh* question No. 3: What is the cost in dollars and cents of this reading program?

We recently conducted a two-year experimental reading program in West Virginia. This program included many ingredients of a good program: listening, speaking, reading, writing activities, paperbacks, kinesthetic approaches, creative activities, listening stations, viewing mechanisms, and reading mechanisms—in other words, the works. Besides all this matter, individual study booths and individual reinforcement activities were provided. This program, however, was determined by the county as being too expensive per pupil. You may say, "This is false economy," and you may be right. Yet if the money isn't there, it is difficult for educators to operate that program.

An excellent research paper could be written by capable educators concerning this particular reading program, yet very few counties in our state could afford the program and maintain the other facets of the curriculum. Perhaps only 20 percent of the school systems in the United States could afford such a program, even with federal monies being provided. In many instances, then, the cost of a reading program becomes the determining factor in acceptance.

And now for *wh* question No. 4: What critical and analytical reading skills should I use in reading this article? In teaching critical reading, I found such analytical reading skills presented as knowing fact from fiction, detecting propaganda, checking accurate sources, having a questioning mind, locating and evaluating information, recognizing connotations or denotations of thought, and having valid information.

As I studied these skills, I realized that if we use even one of these critical reading skills, evaluating information, we cannot be misled by any article. Our need, then, is to become good analytical readers.

In summation, let's look for these items in reading reports on teaching at home or at school: First, consider the writer, his experience and background, his motivation for writing, and the styling and tone of the article; second, consider how much research has been carried on and the *who, where,* and *how many* were involved in the research; third, consider the expense of the program in relation to what the youngsters need in a total curriculum; and finally consider the analytical reading skills needed to be wary of the pitfall of generalizing beyond research data.

The public needs to read critically about reading. Part of the responsibility for their ability to do so rests with reading specialists. We may ask: Have they trained the public to read and evaluate, or does the public say with David, "I believe everything I've read."

The PTA and Reading Instruction

Elizabeth Mallory

THAT JOHNNY AND SUE should learn to read, and read well, has been a prime goal of the PTA since its beginnings in 1897. We have always recognized that in the race of life he who runs must read. We have always worked to assure each child this right and privilege. At the second convention of the National Congress of Parents and Teachers (then the National Congress of Mothers) in 1898, Mary H. Weeks told the assembled parents that "Children love to read stories because they wish to identify themselves with the world. . . . They wish to *know* that they may *be.*" Seventy-one years ahead of time, she was anticipating this year's slogan for National Library Week: "Be all you *can* be—read."

This deep concern of the PTA with children's reading has not lessened through the years. Rather, it has been strengthened and deepened by the organization's experience, by advances in child psychology, and specifically by the growth of scientific knowledge in the area of reading. Moreover, we have given our energies to spreading and implementing this concern until now almost every parent in the land, no matter how underprivileged his own childhood may have been, above all else wants his child to learn to read. The sorry thing is that for many parents this wish remains unrealized.

Indeed the militance of disadvantaged parents often stems from anxiety over their children's lack of reading ability. The parents who demonstrated in New York and other cities over the inadequacy of their children's schools were not, for the most part, protesting discrimination or crowded classes or outmoded buildings or inadequate equipment. They were protesting the sheer fact that their children were not learning to

98

read. In a real sense, then, the crisis in big-city education looms largely as a reading crisis. What is more, it is a crisis we are likely to be facing for some time. Many remedies have been offered, but we have not had time yet to find out which is the right one. And the parents have become impatient. They want Johnny and Sue to learn to read *now*. Who can blame them? They are afraid, and rightly so, that their children will be cut off from earning a decent living and thereby be doomed to the poverty and futility that have frustrated their own lives. They are terrified to think that maybe it will be only in the *next* generation, or the one after that, or one still further postponed that *all* normal children will be taught to read.

One doesn't have to be a poverty-stricken parent to appreciate this kind of anxiety. Nothing in the multimedia mix is yet as powerful as a book that appeals to a child's intelligence and emotions. Yet far too many children of school age are deprived of the ideas and experiences that lie within books by the inability to read. Call this dyslexia or any other term; it is a block to learning that one cannot and must not tolerate. Any child who cannot read at his level of development is an impoverished child, thwarted and hampered—a likely candidate for a desperate and defeated adulthood.

Fortunately, a national assessment of education, which includes assessment of reading ability, is already under way. Moreover, every month, if not every week, there is some national conference going on at which professional people and laymen are coping with reading problems as well as with such issues as funding education, decentralization, and community control. Parent participation is a very important element in these discussions. Whatever role parents play in improving education, whether as paraprofessionals or as volunteer laymen, this much is clear: Parents have the largest stake in education. One of their main concerns—among affluent parents as well as the disadvantaged—is that every child be given the kind of reading instruction and instructional materials that will produce the best results.

As the largest voluntary organization in the United States presenting a cross section of American parents, the National PTA obviously reflects this concern. It realizes that educational inequities exist and that the schools are failing too many of our children—that is, failing to meet their needs. It realizes that some teachers and some librarians are not doing all they can to help children become proficient readers. It also realizes fully that some parents are not doing all they can to prepare their children for reading, the skill on which all learning depends. And I'm not thinking of illiterate, disaffected, or discouraged parents but of those who know better and can do better.

Obviously, only if a boy or girl has progressed to a certain competence

in reading can he hope to advance in his lifework. But the PTA wants
more for children than just the practical advantages of reading. It wants
youngsters to know the lifetime joy that comes from a continuous ac-
quaintance with books. When a child learns to read well, he lays up a
vast store of lasting, deeply satisfying, inexpensive enjoyment for life.
It takes less than a dollar to buy paperbacks that nourish every hobby
and answer every curiosity. It takes no money at all to use the inex-
haustible resources of the public library or to own one's first and most
important credit card—the library card. Reading is a pleasure that never
grows flat, unprofitable, and stale. The rewards of reading only become
richer throughout life.

Thus one of the things the PTA wants for all young people is that they
be introduced to good literature and have ready access to it. To hark
back again to our beginnings, Hamilton W. Mabie told the mothers (and
some fathers, too) who attended the first meeting of our organization
in 1897: "No greater good fortune can befall a child than to be born
into a home where the best books are read, the best music interpreted,
and the best talk enjoyed, for in these privileges the richest educational
opportunities are supplied."

Seven years later, Mrs. Theodore W. Birney, founder of the National
PTA, wrote a book called *Childhood*. This book included a chapter on
"Reading for Children," in which she pointed out how much reading can
mean to a child, and she recommended lists of children's books that had
been prepared by the literature committee of the PTA. She took the quite
modern view that it is an injustice to children to limit their reading to
so-called children's books. While there are many good books written
especially for children, she said, "They have as much right as their elders
to the best books in the world." She also made a point of the importance
of having a good encyclopedia in the home.

The PTA has always deplored efforts to corrupt the intelligence and
spirit of the young by disseminating among them books, magazines, comic
books, films, and radio and TV programs that tend to foster a taste for
violence, obscenity, materialism, and disregard for the rights of others.
A statement by Walter L. Hervey at that first PTA meeting in 1897 could
just as well have been made today:

> The crime of our day against childhood is . . . the placing before it of the
> local, the petty, the commonplace, and the distorted. There are publishers
> who each year place before an undiscriminating public attractive books for
> children, in which charming pictures are unequally yoked with inane read-
> ing matter. . . . They present no "view of life" and are [written] in lan-
> guage which has no literary merit, and which is often distinctly bad.

In the interest of better literature for children the members at this 1897 meeting passed a resolution against literature, billboards, and all other forms of communication that work evil on "the inner developing life of imagery."

In recent years the National PTA, for obvious reasons, has been drawn into the critical arena of young people's freedom to read. As you are all painfully aware, every now and then some irate parent takes issue with teachers who have assigned certain books either for class reading or for reading at leisure. In many instances it isn't a *contemporary* book that creates the ruckus. James R. Squire and Robert F. Hogan, in an article they wrote for *The PTA Magazine* a few years ago, give us further insight into parents' objections to books that teachers have included in their book lists. I quote:

> In the files of the National Council of Teachers of English are reports of efforts to ban *Robin Hood*, because it advocates sharing the wealth and is therefore Communistic; *The Scarlet Letter*, because it deals with adultery; *The King and I*, because it mentions a concubine; a short account of the life of Plato, because he advocated something like free love; the *Odyssey*, because this book from the ninth century B.C. is "non-Christian." One quality of a good book is having something to say. Do not most such books offend someone in some way? If we ban all books that offend anyone, what will be left to read?

A valid question indeed! Although the National PTA does not have a policy statement on censorship, it does have several resolutions on pornography as it affects youths. These hard-hitting statements make good reading. As for censorship, first let me say that the books *adults* should read we gladly leave to their conscience, taste, and, I suppose, to what the Supreme Court of the United States considers prurient. But the question that troubles us greatly is this: Should we and can we censor what our children read?

My answer can be summed up as follows: 1) we couldn't censor our children's reading, even if we wanted to; 2) the best things parents can do is build good literary taste in children from the day they start to read or be read to; and 3) if the student's right to read is not to be put in jeopardy, parents no less than teachers and librarians must be involved in developing the best possible program of literature for children and young people. As Squire and Hogan have pointed out:

> Teachers and librarians in the National Council of Teachers of English look to the National PTA and its local units for joint efforts to reach a common goal—a future generation of adults, solidly grounded in their tradition but not confined to it, intelligently curious, brave enough to ask

questions, and wise enough to seek solutions. . . . The Council knows that no single teacher, no solitary librarian left to fight alone against individual censors or pressure groups can long maintain a broad and solid program in literature. Only with the cooperation of interested parents can the profession work in a climate conducive to this growth.

Certainly most parents do not consider themselves literary experts. Even if some of us were, we still would not have the right to dictate to English teachers what books their students should read. This is a professional prerogative, and the PTA would not think of usurping it.

So are the teaching methods that teachers choose to use in their classrooms. We have a right, however, to expect that our children will learn to read easily, with understanding, and with pleasure and profit. As to what method should be followed to arrive at this happy result, that is a professional question to be answered by professionals—the teachers.

Two issues in reading instruction have been hot for more than a decade and show no signs of cooling off. The first has to do with the word versus phonic method or "look-say" versus "decoding"; the second, with whether children barely past babyhood should be taught to read. I should also mention i.t.a., the medium a number of people claim to be highly successful in teaching children to read and write. It is not my intention to deal with the pros and cons of these issues or to tip my PTA hand one way or the other. The reason I mention them is to make clear the policy of the National PTA in such controversial matters. In the field of reading instruction it is our function, as the PTA conceives it, to bring PTA members accurate information about *various* approaches to reading instruction and encourage sound discussion of these approaches. In this case, the more sound, the less fury. Through *The PTA Magazine* and other PTA channels we have kept our members posted on new trends and experiments in reading instruction and what reading authorities think about them.

For example, Jeanne Chall's *Learning to Read: The Great Debate* was not off the press more than a few weeks before William D. Boutwell gave PTA members a comprehensive report on the book in *The PTA Magazine*. And similarly in past years we discussed other books that stirred up controversy about whether Jerry could read. Boutwell urged PTA members not only to read Chall's book carefully but to discuss it at PTA meetings. To assure an informed and impartial discussion, he suggested recruiting the assistance of a professor of education, one specializing in reading, from a nearby university. It is exciting to speculate on how many people, as a result of PTA effort, increased their vocabulary with such beginning-reading terms as *phonemes* and *graphemes, reversals, norms,* and, of course, *decoding.*

Yes, in the beginning is the word, not only for children but for all of us engaged in lifelong learning. One thing is a certainty, not a speculation: The National PTA has helped the general public understand that many skillful classroom teachers, instead of limiting themselves to one method, actually combine several of the best methods in their teaching of reading.

As for parents' teaching toddlers to read, I well recall that when our official magazine published an article entitled "Little Children Can Learn to Read," by Glenn J. Doman, there was quite a clamor from the opposition that their side should be given equal time. It was. In your hands, partners in the educative process, we parents leave the early or later reading problem. But be sure to let us know—and earlier rather than later—when you have reached a consensus.

On the other hand, we of the National PTA do continuously urge that children be exposed to books just as soon as their eyes and hands can identify them. If we were to isolate the single factor that differentiates between early and late readers, it would not be IQ but rather exposure to books. This fact has been documented repeatedly—and most clearly by Dolores Durkin. The home can give no better service to the school than to assure the child an abundance of books.

The PTA knows well that it is primarily up to parents whether their children become good readers and whether they enjoy reading. One way of accomplishing both aims is the practice of family reading. The bedtime read-aloud story, with Mother and child eagerly looking at the bright pictures, actually serves many developmental purposes. Almost a century ago Birney, in her book *Childhood,* recommended the habit of reading aloud for an hour or two several evenings during the week "as a strong bond for holding a family together."

The PTA Magazine has published countless articles underscoring the role of parents in reading readiness as well as advising them how to select suitable books for children from given lists of good books both classic and modern. Parents throughout the country are grateful to Ruth Gagliardo for her helpful children's book pages which appear monthly in *The PTA Magazine.*

It stands to reason that, from the day it was founded, the PTA has been a strong advocate of both school libraries and public libraries. The National PTA Committee on Reading and Library Service was created in 1898, one of the earliest of the national committees. It is no accident that the successive national chairmen of this committee have done so much for children's reading. They have all been exceptional workers in fields related to books and reading.

One of these exceptional persons is the National PTA president, Elizabeth Hendryson, who some years ago served as national chairman of the Committee on Reading and Library Service. At the 1957 joint meeting of the National Congress and the International Reading Association, Mrs. Hendryson summarized the role of the PTA in promoting library service and in making parents aware of the value of reading. She told how some PTAS work directly with children. For example, they sponsor summer reading programs for boys and girls. Or, where there are no libraries or book stores, PTAS borrow collections of children's books from state and regional libraries or draw up lists of places from which books may be ordered. PTAS work to get bookmobiles to bring books to all children. They also set up parent education discussion groups on children's literature and storytelling, conducted in cooperation with local public libraries. And, of course, they promote the formation of good home libraries by arranging book exhibits and book fairs—all part of the home's reinforcement of reading instructions.

Since confusion arises occasionally about PTA policy on book fairs, it might be well to review the criteria set up by the National PTA to govern book fairs sponsored by local PTAS: 1) Book fairs in local communities should be developed jointly by the PTA, school and public libraries, and bookstores within the community; 2) selection of books should follow the standards recommended by professional librarians and the National Congress of Parents and Teachers; 3) the practice of making books available for purchase at these fairs is not considered a violation of the noncommercial policy if selections are not limited to one publisher or one store in the community (in which there are several stores); and 4) the objective of the book fair should be the bringing of a selection of good books to the attention of parents, teachers, children, and other citizens, and not fund raising for the PTA treasury.

On a national scale, it has been the PTA's constant policy to support public libraries. Our representatives have appeared before various governmental agencies to advocate increases in library budgets. The Library Services and Construction Act, passed by Congress in 1966, was a national project of the PTA for the ten years that it took to get the act passed.

The PTA has always been a strong advocate of school libraries as well. The Board of Managers issued a statement in 1963 advocating the establishment in each elementary school of an adequate central school library under the guidance of a professionally trained librarian.

PTA members have provided important aid to school libraries in both elementary schools and high schools by doing everything from mending old books and helping to catalog new ones to checking out books and manning the school library during the summer so that children will have a handy source of books for their vacation reading.

A nationwide project initiated in 1965 deserves special mention. I refer to the Books for Appalachia project, which the National PTA undertook when asked by the Office of Economic Opportunity to assume leadership in providing much-needed books and magazines for the one- and two-room schools in the far reaches of the Appalachian Mountains. When the project started, the association set its sights on furnishing the area with about one million volumes. By the end of 1965, PTAs had provided 1,100,000 books of many kinds, including reference works such as atlases, encyclopedias, dictionaries, supplementary subject materials, new and imaginative textbooks, poetry, and picture books. These were for children of varying ages and reading ability. In addition, we had built 12,882 bookcase-boxes that were used as carriers for the books and then as bookshelves in the schools.

Now what about the textbooks used in schools? Do we parents have a right to our say about the *quality* of the textbooks? I think so. I think parents have a right to demand that the readers through which a child enters the world of books be logically and coherently written, however simple they may be. We have a right to demand that the content not be so silly, flat, and boring that children are repelled or confused by it or persuaded that reading can never be exciting or fascinating. If some of the greatest books in the world have been written for children, surely some of the worst have also been written for this innocent captive audience. It remains for parents who care about the quality of education to insist that beginning readers everywhere will bring reading pleasure as well as profit to young users.

In 1963 the National Board of Managers, mindful of the need for community involvement in the curriculum, pointed out that "consultations with parents relative to the selection of textbooks may be desirable and useful to the authorities responsible for the textbook selection." The PTA, the statement goes on to point out, fully recognizes that authority to select textbooks rests by law with state or local educational agencies and is usually delegated to the professional staff of the school system. Selection of textbooks is guided by certain policies that define the responsibilities of the school board and of such other persons designated by the board. "Therefore," the statement concludes, "it is appropriate for a PTA, if invited by the proper authorities, to be represented in the reviewing of textbooks or on committees created to advise textbook selection agencies. The PTA should not itself set up a reviewing committee," since this action would be contrary to the noninterference policy of the National PTA.

I must not fail to mention the current PTA Action Program, *Growing Up in Modern America,* with its conclusive evidence of involvement in children's reading; for example, the first priority listed in the Action Program is improving one's school. PTAs are urged to hold meetings at which the principal and other members of the school staff describe the school program. These meetings are based on a survey of what parents want to know about the school. Six examples of what they want to know are cited, and two out of the six deal with reading and instructional materials.

After this discussion of the PTA and reading instruction, I hardly need to assure you that the National PTA is ready, by tradition and conviction and by policy and practice, to work with teachers in every way to enable children to read and read well, so they may truly become all that they can be.

What Parents Can Do for the School

Burley Miller

IT IS A ROUTINE matter to say we are living in a period of change. Such words as "The Challenge of Change," "Resistance to Change," "The Impact of Change," "The Sounds of Change," and "Change in Today's World" are themes used in many organizations. We agree, change is with us. We are involved whether we wish to be or not.

How does change affect what parents can do for schools? Because it is an age of change, everything that parents do must be reflected against a background different from the environment of their youth. Before parents can be effective change agents, they must know what is happening in the schools, specifically the new philosophies of education and the new curriculum developments. Parents must know the meaning of the new math, the linguistic approach to teaching English, modular scheduling, team teaching, ungraded systems, and the cognitive development of children. It is easy to list the many changes, but an understanding of them is difficult. An acceptance of them is generally more difficult.

Americans have been said to be apathetic toward change; we resist it; we are traditional; we refuse to relate to other human beings; we turn our backs; we withdraw; we do not communicate. We appear to listen and accept, but it may be only pretense. We freeze; we build a wall; we are more and more sure we are right.

Teachers may say they have changed their way of teaching. They buy some new equipment—some new audiovisual material, a few new books—and feel they have modernized their method. Close observation indicates they are teaching the same old subject matter the same old way. It takes more than equipment to make a difference.

Change has been accepted in our use of modern conveniences and luxuries. We love our up-to-date automobiles, our larger and faster airplanes, our push-button controlled garage doors, our kitchen and laundry appliances; yet we may vote down a bond levy for new schools. We may secretly feel the old way of teaching the multiplication tables was effective and is good enough for today. Someone has said, "We can put a man on the moon, but we can't change a grading system."

The fact is, however, that in spite of our seemingly innate aversion to change, changes have taken place in school systems. We have many excellent schools with excellent teachers. We are educating more children than we educated in past years and are doing a better job of it. Regardless of the controversy over the "right way" to teach reading, children are learning to read today. Creativity is welcomed. Investigation is encouraged. Experimentation and research continue to seek answers to better ways of teaching and learning.

When parents have carefully scrutinized their own feelings about change and are willing to keep an open mind to new approaches to learning, they are ready to begin to help the schools. First, they can interpret the school program to the community. Most people agree that reading is one of the most, if not the most, important subject to be taught. How well children learn to read is always of prime importance. Parents may be of great help in letting the community know what is really happening in the school reading program. If the i.t.a. system, the code breaking approach, or any other of the many methods now acceptable are being used, they will need favorable reviews for their acceptance. Parents are good communicators with the public because their children are directly involved. Their opinion has credence. It is important, however, that parents become quite knowledgeable about the program before they try to explain it to the public. Observation alone will not be sufficient. Parents need to be instructed by teachers in interpreting the reading process. They must know, for example, not only that a programed approach is being used but how it is used and why it is effective. Knowing about a method, how it operates, and why it is important and then seeing effective results should create an eagerness to want to tell others about it. Parents' enthusiasm about a program should be catching.

Today, as never before, the support of schools by the public is necessary. No school can operate successfully without it. When the community understands and accepts the reading program or any other program in the school and believes it to be good, support will be forthcoming. Therefore, the support that parents are able to secure is of prime importance.

There are many ways parents can help the schools by directly working with their children. Teaching reading is a difficult job in which both the school and the parent can cooperate. The New York City schools have prepared a list of suggestions for parents that seems particularly useful. It was prepared by the Division of Elementary Education, Board of Education of New York City. Here are the instructions to follow:

1. Talk to your child. Research has clearly shown that the baby who is talked to and loved responds and develops more rapidly than one whose physical wants alone are of major concern. Children learn vocabulary very early if they hear it.
2. Listen to your child. The more he talks, the better he is likely to read. Encourage him to read to you. He already should have been instructed that first he reads the story to himself and knows the words and then he reads aloud for others to enjoy. In listening to a child, a parent may become aware of his own lack of knowledge. Recently a child viewing some lobsters in a glass case said, "Daddy, does a lobster ever come out to play on the sand?" Well, does he? Do you know? If you don't, it should be interesting to find out.
3. Read to your child. He will love you for it and also be more eager to read by himself. Reading becomes important.
4. Help him with his reading. Here, again, it is advisable that parents take directions from the teacher. She may suggest you use the methods she uses in the classroom. Usually a safe response when a child does not recognize a word is to say, "What do you think would make sense?" or "What is the initial sound?" Most authorities agree that telling the child a word is acceptable. It keeps the flow of thought from being interrupted, and a word study can be undertaken later.
5. Teach your child how to take care of books. He will learn by seeing you handle a book. Surely you do not turn down corners!
6. Take him on trips. It will not only give him an interest in the world around him but will give him something to talk about. Curiosity will lead to reading to seek more information.
7. Build up a reading atmosphere at home. Have books, magazines, and newspapers available. Tune in on thoughtful programs on TV and radio. Your child may imitate.
8. Encourage him to join and use the public library. Give him help in making his first trip a joy. First impressions may be lasting ones.
9. Buy games and puzzles for your child. Select games that will help reading. Words and letters are generally helpful. Puzzles help with size and shape discrimination.
10. Make up games. Play with rhyming words or naming words that begin with the same sound. Troublesome words may be put on word cards.
11. Buy books for your child. Reading should be fun. To make it so, buy books with a vocabulary he can read and content he likes. Appropriate children's magazines are also good.
12. Praise your child. Don't expect too much. Reading is a difficult task. Telling a word once may not be enough. It may need to be told many, many times. A word of encouragement pays dividends.

13. Keep your child well and rested. An aching tooth or a painful ear-ache are not conducive to reading. Neither can a sleepy child or a hungry child do his best work.
14. Give your child responsibilities. Be sure they are ones he can handle and are acceptable to him. Satisfaction from accomplishment is a good feeling.
15. See that your child has good habits of attendance. Always speak of school as a good place to be. One can't afford to miss what happens.
16. Check your child's report card. Help him with trouble spots. Teacher direction may be necessary for this work. Don't "nag" about grades but find out the cause.
17. Set aside a time for homework and see that there is a comfortable place to do it.
18. Guide your child in better movie going and TV viewing. Teach selec-tivity.
19. Accept your child as he is. Encourage him to improve his work within his ability. Don't compare him with his brothers, with his sisters, or other classmates.
20. Show an interest in the school. Parents and teachers are partners in teaching children to read.

It is known that learning difficulties may arise when children experience some physical or emotional disturbance, are culturally deprived, have been subjected to poor teaching-learning situations, or display an apa-thetic attitude toward school generally. If learning disabilities are identi-fied, correctional programs can be planned. Early identification may pre-vent more problems in later years. In some cases remediation requires a one-to-one relationship that could be performed by parents. For example, volunteer parents have been trained to work with dyslexic children with successful results. Many materials are being published today that can be used successfully by parents with teacher supervision. Marianne Frostig's developmental program in visual perception is an example.

Tutoring is becoming quite popular and may be very helpful. Parents who have time and are qualified, or can become qualified, may give valu-able service to schools.

The importance of the early years of a child's life cannot be overesti-mated. In fact, they have been identified as the critical years. Our gov-ernment, through the work of pediatric researchers in the National Institute of Health, has discovered some highly significant facts: That improper diet before the age of four years can affect height and that after age four little can be done to correct the deficiency; that infants see and discrim-inate almost from birth; and that children who babble and vocalize more at infancy turn out to have higher IQs than the quiet ones. Piaget, the noted Swiss psychologist, points out that only when a child can practice fully his motor-sensory powers can verbal imagery, willpower, and learning abilities grow to full potential in later life. Psychologists are in general agreement that if this early period is not properly filled with things to see, hear, and manipulate and with areas to control, a child's future is irreparably damaged. Missed stages are impossible to make up; overdoses at later stages can never quite do the job.

With the realization that a small amount of educational, parental, and environmental effort may develop a creative adult who has enthusiasm, a will to learn, and inner discipline and emotional stability to handle any social change, parents have a great responsibility to understand and work with young children. Like psychologists, they must try to comprehend each maturation level in a child's development and learn how to create an environment that nourishes growth, wonder, and learning. By doing so, they not only prepare the child for the school to receive him but can have confidence that he is already on his way to realizing his potential. It thus becomes the greatest service a parent can perform for his child and the school.

74127